# THE FRUIT
# OF THE SPIRIT

Books in the Woman's Workshop Series

**Woman's Workshop Series**

# THE FRUIT OF THE SPIRIT

## STUDIES ON GALATIANS 5:22-23

## SANDI SWANSON

**Lamplighter Books** Grand Rapids, Michigan
Zondervan Publishing House

The *Fruit of the Spirit: Studies on Galatians 5:22–23*
Copyright © 1989 by Sandi Swanson
All rights reserved

Previously published as *A Woman's Workshop on the Fruit of the Spirit*

Lamplighter Books are published by the Zondervan Publishing House
1415 Lake Drive, S.E., Grand Rapids, Michigan 49506

ISBN 0-310-52241-2

Edited by Martha Manikas-Foster, John Sloan

*View from the Window at Eragny* by Camille Pissarro
Cover Photo by SUPERSTOCK INTERNATIONAL
Cover Design by *The Church Art Works,* Salem, Oregon

Printed in the United States of America

90  91  92  93  94  95 / CH / 7  6  5  4  3  2

# CONTENTS

## THE BLOOM, THE FRUIT

Men and seed are some the same,
Similar creatures with a different name.

Both need soil and sun to grow . . .

Rain does come and men do cry . . .
But it brings not a gleam,
to the Gardener's eye.

Not the planting, not the strain,
To stop the weeds, to man the hoe . . .

Not the insect, not the fly . . .
That brings a gleam,
To the Gardener's eye.

Strange that men should be as seed,
Needing sun and shunning weed,
By cleansing the plants his care he shows . . .

Gardens grow and gardens die . . .
But it brings not a gleam,
To the Gardener's eye.

Producing what the seed is for,
Live the life that Christ first bore,
Letting bud's full colors loom,
Producing fruit, bearing bloom . . .

To love him back, with a wholehearted try . . .
This brings a gleam to the Gardener's eye.
This brings a gleam to the Gardener's eye.

The bloom brings a gleam to the Gardener's eye.

                                    Jim Swanson

# 1

# THE FRUIT OF THE SPIRIT

In the sagebrush setting of central Oregon, on the half-million-acre Warm Springs Indian Reservation sits Kahnee-ta Lodge. Surrounded by unique Indian sculptures and wood-carvings, several women from my church family gathered together. Some were secretaries, some teachers or managers of their own businesses, while others made raising children their full-time employment. We had gathered together, even in our diversity, for mutual Christian encouragement.

The crisp, cold weather could not chill the warm enthusiasm of our fellowship. We listened intently as the speaker, Myrna Alexander, taught on how God's relationship to the Christian is as a refuge and tower. She exhorted us to *know* God better in order to face trials with a new awareness of God's sovereign shepherding.

As the fireplace sizzled, we sipped hot herb tea leisurely and munched fried Indian bread smothered with deep purple blackberry jam. We warmed our conversation with love and acceptance. Before the bright flames, our friendships deepened as we shared with each other honestly.

The weekend was perfect. No screaming kids. No pressures of a demanding boss or work deadline. No heavy confrontations. However, it came to an abrupt end. At the 12:00 checkout time, we departed through polished, carved wood doors—back to the reality of everyday life.

We inched our way home on the icy road of Mount Hood pass, slowly descending the mountain. My friend Bea and I stopped for a Mexican meal before returning home—our last dinner in tranquil surroundings.

Having eaten our spicy enchiladas and chips, we drove the last miles to the little country town of Sandy, Oregon. This was it. The retreat was over. Back to my "normal" life. Armed with tools from the retreat, I could now successfully face life's pressures, or so I thought.

After I said good-bye to Bea, I hurried in out of the cold. I was greeted by my grinning, dirty-faced two-year-old. His diaper scented the air with an aroma I had not missed during the last three days. The other six boys hovered over me with nonstop questions. I gave my husband, Jim, a quick hello and a peck on the cheek before he dashed out the door for a church leader's meeting.

Popcorn seeds and cornflakes crunched under my shoes as I walked into the kitchen and stared at a sink full of unscraped dishes. I'm sure the boys and Dad did their best at managing the home for the weekend, but the kitchen desperately needed a woman's touch, as did the rest of the house! There were phone messages to be returned, and mountains of laundry to do. My Mexican dinner churned within my stomach, giving me heartburn and a headache. Little by little the "high" of the retreat faded as reality crept in.

What had Myrna said? What was to be my focus? Who could give me joy in my daily circumstances?

I had a rude awakening that brisk, wintry Sunday afternoon. I had known Jesus as the Savior of my life for almost twenty years. Yet, I felt I neither knew God well enough or had the right resources to respond in a godly fashion to that particular chaos.

Therefore, I decided to get to know God better. And I did. The very next day I started a study on the attributes of God.

"But which attributes should I study?" I asked myself. God is so immense, which ones would be practical for me? After thinking for a while I was reminded of the fruit of God's Spirit. I thought about all the beautiful qualities the Spirit bears as mentioned in Gal. 5:22–23—*love, joy, peace, patience, kindness, goodness, faithfulness, gentleness, and self-control.* I decided that if I studied these nine qualities of the Spirit I would more intimately know God himself.

How true it was! After looking in a concordance under each of the nine qualities, I found God to be everything his Spirit produces. I grew in refreshment and inner strength as I studied about how the limitless God has borne this fruit throughout history. From there I learned how eager his Spirit is to grow these very benefits in me, his own child.

This is how *A Woman's Workshop on the Fruit of the Spirit* was planted, and then grew from a seed thought to a rich garden of study. I hope you will find the study to be a growing, fruitful experience as you come to know God better and as you depend on his Spirit to equip you to bear his fruit.

First, let's look at the overview of Galatians where we find the fruit of the Spirit passage.

## OVERVIEW AND INTRODUCTION

**Author:** Paul, an apostle (Gal. 1:1); it was handwritten with the help of an unnamed scribe. We know this because Paul mentions the section he wrote with his own hand (6:11).

**Date:** The date is debated. However, we do know it was written between Paul's first missionary journey (Acts 13) and his death. Therefore, the date is probably sometime between A.D. 52 and 65. For many reasons, an early date between these two dates is more probable.

**To Whom It Was Written:** The Galatians; scholars give two possibilities as to who the Galatians were. The more probable is that they were the believers mentioned in the second missionary journey in Acts 14 ff. These people lived in the Roman province of Galatia, located in central to south central modern-day Turkey, known in biblical times as "Asia Minor." Paul often uses the Roman province names when going into an area.

A less likely possibility is that the Galatians were the Celtic people of northern Turkey who were known as the Gauls.

**Purpose for Writing:** Paul is distressed by a heresy which said that performing works under the Law will commend a person to God. With no qualifications, he strongly argues that grace alone is the means to become right with God.

## THE OUTLINE OF GALATIANS

   I. The Greeting (1:1–5)
  II. Curses for the Perverters of the Gospel (1:6–10)
      (Usually Paul thanks the recipients of his letters here, so you can see the tone of this letter.)
 III. Paul's Personal History (1:11–2:21)
      A. His apostleship divinely sanctioned (1:11, 12)
      B. His God-calling to the Gentiles (1:13–17)
      C. His unquestioned apostleship by Jerusalem apostles (1:18–2:10)
      D. His confrontation with Peter, demonstrating Paul's apostolic authority (2:11–14)
      E. His personal testimony argues against Judaizers (2:15–21)

IV. Paul's Dogmatic Argument (3:1–4:31)
   The argument: Judaistic Christianity (or Christianity
   according to the Law) is inferior to the doctrine of
   faith.
   A. The Christian Galatians are bewitched by return-
      ing to Law (3:1–5)
   B. The faith-blessing of Abraham (3:6–9)
   C. Christ removed the curse of the Law (3:10–14)
   D. God's covenant of promise not voided by the
      Law (3:15–18)
   E. The Law's limited function led the way for
      Christ (3:19–29)
   F. The Law makes slaves, faith makes sons and
      heirs (4:1–7)
   G. Paul's personal appeal against mere ritualism
      and his advocacy for a renewal of their friend-
      ship (4:8–20)
   H. Scriptural allegory (Sarah and Hagar) contrasts
      freedom of Christianity with legal bondage
      (4:21–31)
V. Ethical Exhortations (5:1–6:10)
   The true character of Christian freedom
   A. Circumcision excluded; likewise Judaism (5:1–6)
   B. Condemnation of circumcision teachers (5:7–12)
   C. Liberty in the Spirit bathed in love (5:13–15)
   D. Superiority of freedom of Spirit compared with
      freedom of the flesh (5:16–26)
   E. Spiritual freedoms breed sympathy for burdened
      and liberality in sowing (6:1–10)
VI. Conclusion (6:11–18)
   Handwritten by Paul, contrasting the Judaizer's
   thinking with his own. Gives no personal, final
   greetings.

Now we must zero in on the context of Gal. 5:22–23. Read aloud Gal. 5:16–26.

As you will notice, Paul has contrasted two lists. Often Paul uses lists of words to paint a word picture. In the list of the works of the flesh, he is not really focusing on each individual word (like an outline) but uses the words as a collage to depict the terrible, immoral, insecure, and uncontrollable nature of humans. We will not spend any time dwelling on these words trying to come up with every nuance of meaning. Just read them and say, "What an awful way to live!"

Contrasted with this is the fruit of the Holy Spirit. It is only one fruit with many qualities or benefits. Each one of these qualities is present in the believer as he trusts in Jesus and his free covenant of blessing. It is false to say that you have only some of these qualities. If you are a believer in Christ, you have them all. Maybe not everyone seems to be present, but it is nevertheless. The potential for every one of them is present at all times you are walking (living and trusting) by the Spirit.

Paul is painting a picture of the faithful Christian's potential under the new covenant. A fresh collage develops, one of beauty, control, and security, all polished and poised. The fruit of a life of trusting in Christ and his work puts us right into true kingdom living.

## STUDY QUESTIONS

1. What are the two lists Paul contrasts in Gal. 5:16–26?

v. 19 _____

v. 22 _____

2. a. Which title is plural? _____

b. Which title is singular? _____

**c.** What could be God's reason for inspiring Paul to write "the fruit (not 'fruits') of the Spirit" in singular form? ___

_____

**3.** List each action or characteristic in the passage under the appropriate heading.

| Works of the Flesh* | Fruit of the Spirit |
|---|---|
| | |
| | |
| | |
| | |
| | |

*As you may have noted, the New International Version uses "the acts of the sinful nature" instead of "works of the flesh," as in the King James, American Standard, and Revised Standard Version "deeds." Although "acts" is an accurate translation for the Greek word "ergon," it seems somewhat neutral. "Works" has a better connotation for self-effort and toil, so I chose its title for this study because of its stronger contrast with the fruit of the Spirit.

Think for a moment about "works" and "fruit."

**4.** What words come to mind when you read the word, *works?* _____

_____

**5.** What "pictures" do you see when you consider how fruit grows and what it needs in order to grow? _____

_____

Certainly, a vast difference exists between the works of the flesh and the fruit of the Spirit. The works of the flesh are products of humanity's own fallen nature. The fruit of the

Spirit is produced by the very Spirit of God within the believer.

Yes, the Spirit is in every Christian. The Word tells us that God's Spirit indwells each believer at the point of conversion. Because we are his children, God sends his Spirit into our hearts (Gal. 4:6). We are now his temple, and his Spirit takes up residency in our lives (1 Cor. 3:16, 1 Cor. 6:19, 2 Tim. 1:14, 1 John 4:13). With the promise of God's Spirit comes the power to produce his character, his benefits, and his fruit in our lives.

Can the fruit of the Spirit be counterfeited? It is possible for human effort to counterfeit some aspects of the fruit of the Spirit, but it can never truly produce the Spirit's fruit. But how can we distinguish between the two? The fruit that the Spirit produces gives the glory to God. The woman bearing his fruit does not inwardly puff up and seek praise for herself. She is energized by knowing and trusting her God to dwell in her and produce his qualities in her.

## Reread Gal. 5:24–26

**6.** What "weed" needs to be put to death in order for the Christian to bear the fruit of the Spirit (v. 24)? _____

_____

**7.** Who must work the soil of the believer's heart to enable her to grow fruit (vv. 22a, 25)? _____

_____

Just as natural fruit cannot grow in every climate, the fruit of the Spirit cannot grow in every individual's life or in every church. The Spirit's fruit grows in a climate blessed with an abundance of the Spirit and the Word. This involves yielding to the Word, obedience, prayer, worship, confession, praise, and fellowship with God's people.

In addition to needing the right climate and soil yielded to Jesus, the Gardener must be allowed to weed the garden in order for his fruit to grow.

**8.** What are three specific "weeds" of our sinful nature listed in Gal. 5:26? _____

_____

*The fruit of the Spirit that God produces within the believer is to be absorbed, not just admired and put on display.* Take an illustration from nature's fruit: have you ever tried to keep an attractive, luscious fruit basket on your kitchen table for more than a few weeks? Within just a few days something of beauty becomes an inn for fruit flies and little hairy, gray mold. Likewise, the Spirit's fruit must not be tucked away in your heart, but must be fed to sad, love-starved, stressed-out people. You must not bear fruit solely for your own consumption; no, you must bear fruit so that all will be nourished and helped and, most of all, so that Christ will be honored and glorified.

Let's look briefly at the importance of the word *fruit* in the Bible. In the original language, the word for fruit is *karpos,* which meant any kind of fruit. It was even used to refer to a baby, as in "the fruit of the womb," although it most frequently meant the product of the fruit tree or vine. In Gal. 5:22 it is used figuratively as the "result, outcome, or product" of the Spirit.

Fruit bearing is an old metaphor with its roots deep in the soil of the Old Testament. Read Psalm 1. This passage speaks of the blessed man (or woman) who bears fruit in season. John used it in chapter 15 of his gospel. Christ is the Vine and those who acknowledge him are his fruit-bearing branches. The Lord, in Matt. 7:16, said that a tree can be recognized by the fruit that it bears. Therefore, if these qualities of the fruit of the Spirit are present in your life, you are identified with God and his ways, and receive his benefits.

**9.** After finishing this introductory material, what personal goals do you have for this workshop? _____

_____

_____

_____

## MEMORY VERSE

Each week there will be a memory verse to learn. Hiding God's Word in the mind and heart enables the believer to successfully deal with life's demands. Therefore, with another person in your study, become mutually accountable for learning the memory verses. The Word, stored within, will help you grow. As you may have guessed, the memory verses for this week are:

> But the fruit of the Spirit is love, joy, peace, patience, kindness, goodness, faithfulness, gentleness and self-control. Against such things there is no law.
>
> Gal. 5:22–23

## GEMS

Also, at the end of each lesson you will find an area marked GEMS. This stands for "**G**od **E**nlightening **M**y **S**tudy" and it is space for you to add any other material pertinent to that week's study.

*A Woman's Workshop on the Fruit of the Spirit* is an exciting, energizing study that will encourage and enrich your growth in godliness. In each of the next eleven weeks you can look forward to learning about God through a specific fruit of his Spirit. We will begin the next two lessons with love. Love is the most important of all.

| GEMS |
| --- |
| |

# 2

## LOVE

In the 1960s, a popular song included the lyrics, "What the world needs now is love, sweet love." Yes, how true, the world did and still does need love, yet people often look in the wrong places for genuine love. Blinded by their own self-centeredness, they often refuse to see the greatest love relationship of all: the love of God for his people.

In this lesson we will look briefly at the background of the word *agapē*, used in Gal. 5:22 for love.* Then we will study love through the actions of God. We will also see that although sometimes taught as such, the God of the Old Testament is not a *wrathful* God who was replaced by a *loving* God in the New Testament. No, we will see how God's love has been constant and faithful throughout history.

*Love is number one. God made no mistake in instructing the apostle Paul to list love first in the qualities of the fruit of the Spirit, for each remaining quality is summarized and purified in the concept of love. Because there is such a wealth of study relating to God's love, we will be spending two lessons on this attribute.

It is through this constant, faithful, loving God that we can truly love others. As you study this very crucial attribute of our God, may he clothe your being with his love.

## BACKGROUND

The word used in Gal. 5:22 for love is *agapē*. *Agapē* in the New Testament represents a love which is unconditional. This love seeks only the highest good for another, no matter how it is treated. Although this word rarely appears in any secular Greek writings of biblical days, it appears over sixty times in Paul's letters.

This quality of unconditional love was foreign to the pagan mind. Aristotle believed that only the deserving should be loved, and Plato held the belief that love is only for the lovely. Jesus Christ, our true teacher, recognized this when he said, "If you love only those who love you there is no reward, because even the taxgatherers do the same thing." Here Jesus simply stated the truth—that human nature gives conditional love.

Although the word *agapē* was sometimes used to mean a self-indulgent love in the Greek Old Testament (Judg. 16:4), every occurrence of *agape* in the New Testament refers only to the highest form of love. Yes, by New Testament times this word had been dusted off and polished to become the very kind of love God modeled.

God's love is unconditional, sacrificial, and a direct act of his will. It is not the warm, gushy feelings that ooze from the pages of a romance novel, nor the sensual arousals of the soap operas' unfaithful lovers, nor the warm fuzzy yet fickle feelings of a senior high school sweetheart. No, God's agape love is unique. Let's look at the following passages to see how our great God loved, and continues to love, his people.

## STUDY QUESTIONS

**1. a.** Read the passages below and list who God loved, and why or how God loved.

|  | Who | How or Why |
|---|---|---|
| Deut. 7:6–9 |  |  |
| Neh. 9:16–21 |  |  |
| Jer. 31:1–6 |  |  |
| Zeph. 3:14–17 |  |  |
| John 3:16 |  |  |
| Rom. 5:5–8 |  |  |
| Gal. 2:20 |  |  |
| Eph. 2:4–9 |  |  |

**b.** After reading the above passages, list below the characteristics of God's love. Share at least one with your group. _____

**2.** King David, known as a man after God's heart, praised God for his love. Even in unpleasant circumstances, David focused on God and his great love. Study at least three of the following passages to gain a greater appreciation for the kind of God who exists. (Note: The word "love" here is a synonym to *agape* that has strong implications of "faithfulness" and "loyalty" based on God's covenant in the Old Testament. Covenants change, but not God's character.)

Ps. 25:4–7; 26:2–3; 31:7–8, 21; 59:16; 69:13–16; 86:5, 13–15; 103:6–8; 145:8–9.

**3.** After studying the Old Testament and New Testament passages, along with David's view of God, write your own definition of God's love. _____

_____

Have you personally experienced God's love? Have you experienced the refreshment of a cleansed heart through the acceptance of God's greatest act of love? It is a revolutionizing truth that God loved the world and gave his only Son to die in order to bridge the gap between the holy God and a sinful person. It is my prayer that you know this truth. If you have personally believed in this act of God, then you are empowered by God's Spirit.

The following passages relate to God's followers' love. Remember, this love can only be cultivated through the empowerment of God's Spirit living in you.

**Read Matt. 5:43–48**

**4.** Whom are Jesus' followers supposed to love? _____

**5.** Why are we instructed to love them? _____

_____

## Read John 13:34–35

**6.** What new command did Jesus give? _____

_____

**7.** Whose love was to be modeled? _____

**8.** Why did Jesus command it? _____

_____

## Read John 14:15–21

**9.** If a person loves Christ, what will that person do? _____

_____

**10.** What did Jesus promise to give to those who love him (see v. 16)? _____

_____

**11.** What promise is there to those who love God? _____

_____

From these passages we learn that God faithfully loves his people. First of all, he displayed a loyal love to the nation of Israel, and through them he promised a Savior for the entire world. He sent Jesus, his only Son, in a truly sacrificial act of restoring his love relationship with humanity. By accepting Jesus' words, a person has the promise of the Holy Spirit's indwelling and the ability to be a Spirit-controlled lover.

Remember, the productivity of our lives is rooted in our relationship with God. We cannot bear fruit alone, just as a branch cannot bear fruit without the vine and the roots. God's character will flow through us as we pursue knowing him, as we actively reach out to the relationship God has already initiated and established. As our branches are nourished with his ways, we will find opportunities to apply what we've learned to other relationships. We must allow God to Son-ripen our characters and allow Jesus to water and prune our lives for his glory. This takes time—the growing season of life—and soil that is yielded and tilled with his Word. Instead of seeking the product, the fruit of love, we must seek the Source, God himself.

## APPLICATIONS

**12.** Take a few moments to meditate on God's love. Praise God by publicly declaring how he has shown you that he loves you. _____

_____

**13.** Because God's love is so great towards us, we should all the more love him in return. We have learned that one way to love God is to be obedient to his words. Ask God to reveal an area of your life in which you are stubbornly refusing to obey him, and make note of that area on the lines below. Ask his Spirit to help you respond obediently in this area. _____

_____

_____

**14.** Ask God to stretch you in the area of love. We have learned that love is to be the Christian's trademark, so ask God to reveal one person in your life that you need to love unconditionally, such as a demanding boss, a selfish child, an unresponsive husband, a meddling in-law, or an angry teenager. Choose to love this person this week. Afterwards, write down at least one way you expressed love to them. ____

## MEMORY VERSE

> But you, O Lord, are a compassionate and gracious God,
> slow to anger, abounding in love and faithfulness.
>
> Ps. 86:15

| GEMS |
| --- |
|  |

# 3

## MORE LOVE

In my exposure with normal children, troubled teens, and mentally retarded youth, it is easy to see the effect of love—or the lack of it. Children desperately need a listening ear to quiet their fears. They need the warmth of a snug hug. They need a firm, consistent hand of discipline. They also need steady spiritual direction and guidelines, whether they outwardly show their approval for them or not. They need the stable security of an adult who really loves them in actions—not just words.

Yes, let's face it: whether you are a troubled teen, a mentally retarded individual, or a stable grown-up considered "normal," we all need love. And God fills that need by showing us his unconditional love. This chapter speaks of the loving care of God as our parent. May your study of this prominent character quality of God liberate you to be a Spirit-controlled lover.

## BACKGROUND

If you did not work through lesson 2, which was the first chapter on love, read through the background on agape love, found at the beginning of that chapter. This will acquaint you with the meaning of the word.

Remember, agape love is a slow-bearing fruit. It is not the easy or the natural way to love. It takes time to develop this act of your will. But God has grown this love before us and therefore it is on his Spirit we must depend to cultivate agape in our lives.

## STUDY QUESTIONS

### Read 1 John 4:7–21

**1.** Where does true love come from? _____

_____

**2.** What was the instrument through which God showed us his love? _____

_____

**3.** Who makes the Christian's love complete, and through what source is it made complete (vv. 12–13)? _____

_____

**4.** What does God's love prepare us for (v. 17)? _____

_____

**5.** How does experiencing God's love affect our level of fear? _____

_____

**6.** What measuring stick is given to measure whether we are experiencing God's love and therefore loving God in return? _____

_____

_____

**Read Rom. 8:31–39**

**7.** List all the situations that God says cannot separate you from his love. _____

_____

_____

**8.** How does this truth affect your life? _____

_____

**Read Heb. 12:1–6**

**9.** What does God do because he loves his children? _____

_____

**10.** How are we to respond to God's discipline? _____

_____

**11.** Describe an incident in which God disciplined you. How did you feel about his discipline when you went through it? How did you feel when you completed the process? _____

_____

_____

**Read 1 John 3:16–24**

**12.** How did Jesus show us he loved us? _____

_____

**13.** What more is required of a Christian's love than just words? _____

_____

**14.** What would you say about the love of a particular local church who had some members who were going hungry? _____

_____

_____

**15.** Why is obedience important when you love someone?

_____

**16.** What helper did God give us to enable us to live out love in our lives (v. 24)? _____

_____

The Christian woman has been instructed to love. But how are we to love? A popular chapter in the Bible, often referred to as the "love chapter" gives us insight into what godly love is all about. Read it and discover new ways to love.

**Read 1 Cor. 13:1–13**

Meditate on this beautiful love passage. Read it at least two more times.

**17.** Write down all the characteristics of love that you find in this passage.

Love is                                    Love is not

_____

_____

_____

_____

**18.** Rewrite these verses with synonyms or word pictures to help you develop a broader view of what this passage is teaching. _____

_____

_____

_____

_____

## APPLICATIONS

What a mouthful! There is so much written about God's love, that even in two chapters it is difficult to discuss everything. These are the central points of this lesson: God demonstrated his love first, to an undeserving people. God's love is available to all who believe and once it is accepted, nothing can separate a believer from it. Because God's love is inseparable from us, there should be no crippling fear in our lives. God's love remains true to his holy character and therefore brings discipline to the wayward child. The Spirit liberates a Christian to love in action, not in lofty, spineless, sentimental words.

Where do we go from here?

**19.** Write a love letter to God. Express to him your deep appreciation for showing you his love. _____

_____

_____

_____

_____

_____

_____

**20.** Love is action! Ask God to direct you to some body member in need. Lovingly share meeting this need. _____

_____

_____

**21.** Ask God to reveal an area in which you are fearful and note what it is on the lines below. Ask God to envelop this fear with his love. May you daily practice this week to give this fear to him. _____

_____

_____

_____

**22.** Perhaps you are in the process of being disciplined by God. Submit to his discipline and focus on his reason for disciplining you: you are his child and he loves you and wants you to stay near him.

**MEMORY VERSE**

> This is love: not that we loved God, but that he loved us and sent his Son as an atoning sacrifice for our sins.
>
> 1 John 4:10

## GEMS

# 4

## JOY

Fired! That word stung, cutting deep into Betty's self-worth. As the reality of those words slapped her in the face, unmanageable tears trickled down her cheeks. Her face flushed as her boss grappled for words of consolation. "After all, it's not the end of the world," her boss said.

No, it wasn't the end of the world, but who's going to pay next month's rent? And, the Visa card is charged to the limit and needs to be paid this month. The idea of hunting down another job made Betty's blood pressure soar. As she walked out the revolving door onto the crowded sidewalk, worry, feelings of inferiority, and the frustrations of failure loomed overhead. She was depressed and despairing. Joy was nowhere to be found, or was it?

We can find joy even in the midst of defeats and disappointments, and in this study we will see how. We will look at Old Testament and New Testament examples of joy.

We will see the radiant expression of God's presence flowing in his people. We will also see how we can increase one another's joy. Hopefully, you'll discover the secret to "Be joyful always" (1 Thess. 5:16).

## BACKGROUND

In the New Testament, the Greek word *chara,* meaning "joy," is mentioned sixty times. The related verb, *chairo,* meaning "to rejoice," is listed seventy-two times. By the numerous occurrences of joy, you can see the importance of this fruit in a believer's life.

Christian *chara* is not dependent on outward circumstances. It is the inward gladness of heart that comes from knowing and experiencing the presence and perspective of God. It is the presence of God within—expressing his character outwardly—even in times of great difficulty and disappointment.

## STUDY QUESTIONS

**1.** Look up the following verses to see who is the source of joy.

1 Chron. 16:7–36 (In v. 27, a synonym to *chara* is used.) _____

_____

Ps. 16:11 _____

Ps. 43:4 _____

**Read Rom. 15:13**

**2.** List two things God desires to bestow on believers. _____

_____

**3.** What is the prerequisite of being filled with joy? _____

_____

**4.** Who empowers the believer to be filled with joy and hope? _____

_____

**Read Ps. 21:1–7**

**5.** Why did David rejoice? _____

_____

**6.** What key is found in v. 7 enabling David to experience joy in God's presence? _____

_____

**Read Ps. 51:1–15**

**7.** According to the heading, what sinful situation did David find himself in? _____

_____

**8. a.** Before David requested joy (vv. 8, 12), what did he ask from God? _____

_____

**b.** How do you think forgiveness and joy relate? _____

_____

**c.** Can there be joy when you continue in sinful patterns? _____

_____

**9. a.** After David asks God to restore the joy of his salvation, what does David plan to do (v. 13)? _____

_____

**b.** What is the relationship between God-inspired joy and evangelism? _____

_____

_____

**10.** Now let's look at the lives of the Israelites. Look up the following verses and note what specific things gave the Israelites joy. (Some independent historical backgrounds on these texts would be helpful.)

Deut. 16:13–15 _____

_____

1 Kings 8:65–66 _____

_____

2 Chron. 30:21–27 _____

_____

Ezra 6:22 _____

_____

Neh. 8:10–17 _____

_____

From these Old Testament references, we discover that God is the focus of joy. There is joy in praise. There is joy in forgiveness. There is joy in obedience such as the Israelites experienced as they renewed the feast celebrations, dedicated the temple, and renewed the reading of God's Word.

Now let's look at the New Testament.

**11. a.** The gospels record new reasons to rejoice. Read the following references and note why.

Luke 2:8–12 _____

_____

Matt. 28:5–8 _____

_____

Luke 24:50–52 _____

_____

**b.** Who is mentioned in all three passages? Now you know where your focus must be! _____

_____

To finish our Scripture study, let's look at many joy exhortations from the New Testament.

**Read John 15:9–17**

**12.** What were the disciples told to do (vv. 9–10)? _____

_____

**13.** What does our great Teacher state as the reason for talking to his disciples (v. 11)? _____

_____

**14.** How does obeying God's commands and remaining in Christ's love relate to complete joy? _____

_____

_____

**Read 2 Cor. 6:3–10**

**15.** What were Paul and Timothy able to do even in the midst of trials (v. 10)? _____

_____

**16.** Through Whom was this possible (vv. 6–7)? _____

_____

### Read Phil. 2:1–2

**17.** What did Paul request that the Philippians do to make his joy complete? _____

_____

**18.** How does being like-minded, having the same love, and being one in Spirit and purpose affect the joy of your women's Bible study? _____

_____

_____

### Read 1 Peter 1:3–9

**19.** Should trials have any effect on your joy (vv. 6–8)? ____

_____

**20.** How does your love and belief in Christ give you inexpressible and glorious joy? _____

_____

**21.** How does heavenly-mindedness, rather than temporal-mindedness, produce joy in times of trial? _____

_____

### Read 3 John 3–4

**22.** How did John, the elder, receive joy? _____

_____

We have looked at numerous passages. Let's summarize our discoveries.

First of all, we must acknowledge that joy comes from God. God's people can maintain joy through trusting and having clean hearts. Obedience to God's Word and commands, praise, and food celebrations were actions which produced joy in the Old Testament.

The New Testament focuses on Christ's birth, death, resurrection, and ascension as reasons to rejoice. Paul taught that if the Christian's focus is on God and not on temporal, earthly goals, then the Christian can truly rejoice always. Yes, although joy can be an involuntary emotional expression of God working in your life, often joy is a mindset. A mindset that chooses to trust, chooses to cast all worldly concerns on the Master Sustainer, chooses to release joyrobbers to God's care.

We also looked at oneness in Spirit and purpose, as well as walking in the truth, as ways to bring joy to our spiritual leaders. Yes, joy is linked with our ministry to others; in seeing our heavenly investments flourish (1 Thess. 2:19–20).

## APPLICATIONS

**23.** Focus on God. Praise him for the internal happiness he has given you in Christ. Praise him for the forgiveness he dearly bought with his blood. Praise him for his Word, which (if studied) brings joy.

**24.** Search your heart. Confess any known sin. Sin prevents inner joy from reigning.

**25.** Analyze your women's Bible study. Are you one in Spirit and purpose? Ask God to unite you in love in order to increase the joy of your study time.

**26.** Write a letter of encouragement to your spiritual "parent" or leaders. Plant the seed of joy in his/her heart by letting that person know you are "walking in the truth."

**27.** Take note during this week of which circumstances rob you of joy. What will be your plan of attack so that you might fight off depression and replace it with inner joy? When clouds of gloom and despair rain on you, what "umbrella" will protect you from depression? Write down the victory steps which lead to joy. ─────────────────

───────────────────────────────────────────

───────────────────────────────────────────

───────────────────────────────────────────

**MEMORY VERSE**

Rejoice in the Lord always. I will say it again: Rejoice!

Phil. 4:4

(Remember, according to Phil. 1:13, these words were written by a man held in bondage.)

| GEMS |
| --- |
|  |

# 5

## PEACE

It's been one of those days. The phone keeps on ringing, the children keep on fighting, and on the counter lays the pot roast, charred to a crisp. The dog just messed on the freshly shampooed carpet, your husband called to say he's been delayed, and the dinner guests will arrive in barely thirty minutes.

As you hurriedly remove the last electric roller from your tangled hair, you wonder why your knotted stomach aches and your head pounds. Can there be relief without Rolaids or tranquility without tranquilizers?

Without the help of pills, can the Christian woman really find inner peace to sustain her even in a frustrating, tension-filled day? The Word of God says, "Yes!" Through the Spirit of God she can have true tranquility that transcends trials.

So, stop. Grab a breather from your busy schedule. Take a deep breath, kick off those shoes and snuggle up in a comfortable chair with God's Word. Relax. As you read, absorb the truths of God's peace, and discover the biblical principles for practical peace. *Then* when "one of those days" rears its ugly head, you'll be better equipped to be at peace.

## BACKGROUND

The ancient world yearned for peace even as the world seeks it today. Philosophers thought and wrote much about it, and classical Greek thought had certain recurring ideas about it. Greek thinkers believed that in order to attain peace, the following were required:

The death of emotion (apathy)
The elimination of desire
Indifference
Total self-sufficiency

Yet, the fresh wind of God's Spirit came and challenged the suggestions above. New Covenant peace is:

Caring, not apathy
Feeling and desire, but held under control
Involvement, not detachment
Being under control, yet dependent on God to make the
    difference

In the New Testament *eirēnē* is the Greek word for peace. *Eirēnē,* pronounced something like the name "Irene," occurs over eighty-five times, and an additional seven times in verbal form or compound words. It is included in every New Testament book except 1 John, usually occurring as part of the greeting.

The apostle Paul used *eirēnē* in a very special greeting. He melded the standard Greek greeting "grace to you" with the Hebrew greeting, "peace to you." By doing so, he formed a truly unique Christian greeting to demonstrate that the Jew and the Gentile were now one—now able to be at peace with one another. This greeting, "Grace to you and peace from God" is found over and over in Paul's letters.

The concept of peace has a great Hebrew heritage. The Hebrew is *shalom,* which can mean simply "hello" or "how are you." However, it can also mean more than just the absence of trouble or war; it also expresses the positive hope and prayer that one may enjoy all good gifts and blessings from the almighty God. Therefore, as you study peace, keep in mind its hopeful aspects.

Christian peace is defined as "the God-given ability to develop and maintain right relationships, not detachments, in every sphere of life." This means with God, others, and yourself. Christian peace encourages right relationships— first of all with God, then with people and within yourself.

## STUDY QUESTIONS

### GOD'S PEACE

**1.** Study the following verses. Note the attribute of God that is listed in each verse, as well as the context.

|  | Attribute | Context |
|---|---|---|
| Rom. 15:33 |  |  |
| 1 Cor. 14:33 |  |  |
| 2 Cor. 13:11 |  |  |

|  | Attribute | Context |
|---|---|---|
| Phil. 4:9 |  |  |
| 1 Thess. 5:23 |  |  |
| 2 Thess. 3:16 |  |  |

**2.** The previous question reveals that God has a reputation of peace. Discover from the following verses the specific acts God did to display his peace. How did God establish peace between the Jew and the Gentile?

**a.** Rom. 5:1–2 _____

_____

**b.** Col. 1:13–20 _____

_____

**c.** Eph. 2:11–18 _____

_____

Now that God has been identified as the author of peace, study the following Scriptures pertaining to personal peace.

## PERSONAL PEACE
### Read aloud John 14:25–27

Jesus served the Last Supper (Passover meal), washed his disciples' feet, and then spoke intimately to his disciples. As he spoke, he gave the promise of peace.

**3. a.** Whom did God send to remind (or teach) his disciples of the promised peace? _____

_____

**b.** Is he still with us today? _____

**4.** Jesus said his peace was not like the world's peace. In John 14:27, Jesus gives his disciples peace and then admonishes them to void their hearts of two feelings. What are the two feelings, and how do you think they relate to peace?

**a.** _____

_____

**b.** _____

_____

### Read aloud Isa. 26:1–4

**5.** What does God, through the prophet Isaiah, promise to the steadfast, trusting mind? _____

_____

**6.** Define *steadfast* and *trusting*. _____

_____

**7. a.** Who is the focus of the steadfast, trusting mind? _____

_____

**b.** What stable and firm "picture" do we have of God in v. 4? _____

_____

### Read aloud Rom. 8:5–8

**8.** What two minds are listed in this passage?

a. _____

b. _____

**9.** What are the results of the mind being controlled by each of the following:

a. the sinful nature = _____

b. the Spirit = _____

**10.** How does making the choice to live by your sinful nature or by the Spirit affect whether or not you have peace in your life? _____

_____

## PEACE WITH EACH OTHER
### Read aloud Rom. 12:17–21

**11.** What is the context of "living at peace with everyone"—what must be avoided in order to keep peace with all people? _____

_____

**12.** Is there any situation in which the believer *should* retaliate? _____

_____

**13.** Who will take care of the unjust situation (v. 19)? _____

_____

### Read aloud Rom. 14:17–21

**14.** What issue is Paul addressing in this passage? _____

_____

**15.** What are the three qualities of the kingdom of God?

a. _____

**b.** _____

**c.** _____

**16.** Who gives these benefits (v. 17)? _____

_____

**17.** What are two aims for the believer in the body of Christ (v. 19)?

**a.** _____

**b.** _____

What can we learn from this study on peace? First of all, we can know from the Bible that God is the believer's source of peace. His reconciliatory actions through Christ's work on the cross enable the believer to experience peace—peace with her Creator, peace with others, and peace with herself.

Even though the Spirit lives within the believer, the Christian woman has many choices. She can live by the Spirit or she can be pulled another way by her sinful nature. She can choose to focus on her circumstances or she can focus on the "Everlasting Rock." She can be a stumbling block and seek her own revenge, or she can depend on God to guide her daily actions and to take care of any unjust situation according to his timetable. All of these choices will affect her level of peace.

## APPLICATIONS

Let's look at some application questions to help you bear the fruit of peace in your life.

**18.** Stop and think about the tremendous price God paid to bring peace to individuals in our world. If you have personally trusted Christ as your Lord and Savior, take time now to praise God for his provision of peace. If you have not yet acknowledged Christ as your Savior, you may want to consider further Col. 1:13–20.

**19.** On a scale of one to ten (with one meaning you are pushing the panic button and ten meaning you have perfect peace), where are you right now?

| 1 | 2 | 3 | 4 | 5 | 6 | 7 | 8 | 9 | 10 |
|---|---|---|---|---|---|---|---|---|----|

Take a moment and ask God to reveal which areas are robbing you of the Spirit's peace and note them below. Possibly it's an unjust situation, or it's an improper focus. Commit these areas to the "establisher" of peace. _____

_____

_____

**20.** Evaluate the following situations and circle the answer or answers that best describe the way you might respond.

**a.** A demanding boss presses you with a hard deadline. You would

    **1)** feel martyred.

    **2)** want to say you couldn't do it, but lack the courage to say it.

    **3)** complain to fellow workers about the unsympathetic boss you all have to suffer under.

    **4)** mutter negative comments about the boss under your breath.

    **5)** seek to focus on God to enable you to finish the task and keep you from becoming too uptight.

**b.** A family member is late from work and the roads are icy. You

**1)** let your mind wander, imagining all sorts of accidents involving your loved one.

**2)** eat half a dozen chocolate chip cookies to console yourself as you wait.

**3)** call a friend and ask for her support in prayer.

**4)** become increasingly nervous, biting your fingernails and screaming at other family members.

**5)** meditate on Ps. 46:1 or on another verse to help maintain a peaceful attitude.

**c.** Your women's Bible study has dissension. Last week at a special social time, one of the newer women brought a beverage spiced with alcohol. Some of the members were really offended. You, as the hostess will

**1)** ignore the situation because you never have been very good at dealing with controversy. Time will heal the wound, you tell yourself.

**2)** tell the group that the others just had a "holier-than-thou" attitude, so you don't care if they come back.

**3)** call the offended members immediately. Ask for their forgiveness for making them stumble. Truthfully tell them how much you value their friendship and hope that peace can be restored to the group for the sake of Christ.

**4)** disband the Bible study in your house.

**d.** Your neighbors are loud and noisy, their children disrespectful and disruptive. You

**1)** invite them over for a cup of coffee and strudel and discuss with them some of your concerns.

**2)** pretend you are not home when the children knock on your door.

3) put up a "For Sale" sign, and make plans to move to the country.

4) invite the children in for some freshly baked chocolate chip cookies. Lay down the law on what kind of house rules you and your children live by and tell them they are welcome to visit but you will expect them to abide by your guidelines.

21. Recognize the times you are especially uptight this week and why. Then meditate on Phil. 4:6–7. Try to apply these verses to your specific stressful situations. Plan your attack, and use Scripture in your fight. Satan loves for Christians to be so bogged down that we cannot be effective witnesses for Christ.

| Circumstance | Response |
| --- | --- |
| | |
| | |
| | |
| | |

### MEMORY VERSE

Do not be anxious about anything, but in everything, by prayer and petition, with thanksgiving, present your requests to God. And the peace of God, which transcends all understanding, will guard your hearts and your minds in Christ Jesus.

Phil. 4:6–7

| GEMS |
| --- |
|  |

# 6

## PATIENCE

Sheryl was off and running to another district managers' meeting. Fumbling with the old tattered umbrella that never went up when she wanted it to, Sheryl stepped out into the Northwest rain, the sidewalk complete with a puddle for her every step. As she glanced at her watch, she realized that she was already running ten minutes behind schedule. Where did her directions to the meeting go? And where was the briefcase full of computer printouts of stats? And why did that car have to speed through that puddle, splattering mud on her off-white skirt?

"Great!" she said after retrieving her stats, finding the directions, and rubbing out the mud streaks as best she could. But now where were her keys? After fumbling around until she found them, she climbed into her car, dripping wet. Why didn't the car ever start on the first turn of the ignition?

Finally the lousy engine started, but why did every traffic signal greet her with red? And why did the policeman have to look up at the precise moment she went through the intersection? Hadn't the light been amber just a second ago?

Managing to say a friendly good-bye to the officer, Sheryl started off again. Now running twenty-five minutes late, she hurriedly buried the $57 fine deep in her purse. Shivering in her wet clothes, she turned on the heater only to be greeted by a blast of cold air. The thermostat must be sticking. Why can't things just work like they should?

Finally she arrived at 1040 N.W. Morrison. After circling the block three times, she pulled up to a vacant parking spot but then, out of seemingly nowhere, a blue Spitfire pulled in. She made five more trips around the block before settling for a tight spot three blocks away. Not just tight, it was *too* tight, she realized, as she heard the crunch of metal. Another fender bender! That meant another call to the insurance agent. Sheryl could see the dollar signs rising.

At least it's not raining, she thought, as she hurried up the street. Upon arriving, the receptionist told her that the meeting location had been changed. The woman sweetly asked, "Didn't your office relay the message? I called them this morning." At that point Sheryl felt like redecorating the office by throwing a slender vase of daffodils against the ivory wall. *Patience, patience, patience*, she thought, while she clenched her jaw.

Although somewhat exaggerated, we're each confronted with similar ordeals. Maybe you're home with two children still in diapers, or maybe you've been left with the total care of an aging parent, or perhaps you are in the midst of a debilitating disease yourself. Wherever we are in life, we all need a shield of patience. With an armor of patience we can more successfully face life's battles.

So even if you have heard the saying, "Don't ever *pray* for patience," that's exactly what this lesson is all about. The Spirit is eager to teach us about our ever-patient God, and he is willing to develop this aspect of himself in your life. Hang in there, the trials may be abundant this week, but so also his fruit!

## BACKGROUND

In the context of Gal. 5:22, the word for patience is *makrothumia*. This noun, along with a corresponding verb *makrothumeō*, is listed twenty-four times in the New Testament. *Makrothumia* conveys the idea of long-suffering, patience, or tolerance. It is the active quality of putting up with other people, even when patience is sorely tried.

The history of the word puts together two Greek words: *Macro* meaning to "be far" and *thumos* meaning "anger."* So, the placing of anger on the back burner instead of letting it boil over is at least part of the New Testament idea. One who keeps anger away from her heart's door exudes steadfastness, endurance, and the ability to wait.

## STUDY QUESTIONS

Let's look first at God's example of patience.

**1.** Read the following verses. Note who said God is patient (slow to anger), when he said it, and how God showed that patience.

---

*This breakdown of word parts is for illustrative purposes and is not a guide to meaning.

| | Who | When | How |
|---|---|---|---|
| Exod. 34:4–7* | | | |
| Neh. 9:16–18, 29–31 | | | |
| Joel 2:12–13 | | | |
| Jonah 3:10–4:2 | | | |
| 1 Tim. 1:12–16 | | | |
| 2 Peter 3:9, 15 | | | |

*These thoughts also appear in Num. 14:18; Ps. 86:15, 103:8, 145:8.

Share with your group one discovery you made in the above passages.

**2. a.** The book of Proverbs gives insight on the quality of patience. Study the following five passages and note the importance of patience. Write down the kind of people who characterize patience and, in those verses that supply the information, contrast them with those who don't.

|  | Patient | Impatient |
|---|---|---|
| Prov. 14:29 | | |
| Prov. 15:18 | | |
| Prov. 16:32 | | |
| Prov. 19:11 | | |
| Prov. 25:15 | | |

**b.** What are some results of being patient? _____

_____

**Read Ps. 40:1–3**

**3.** What did David do? _____

_____

**4.** What did God do?

**a.** _____

**b.** _____

**c.** _____

**d.** _____

**e.** _____

_____

**f.** _____

_____

**5.** What can be the outcome of God's children waiting patiently on God? _____

_____

_____

### Read Heb. 6:13–15

**6.** How did Abraham respond to God's promises (v. 15)?

_____

**7.** How did God respond to Abraham's patience? _____

_____

**8.** Consult a Bible commentary to see how long Abraham waited for a descendant once God promised to make him the father of a great nation. How does knowing this help you when you feel God is not answering you fast enough? _____

_____

**9.** Let's look at some New Testament exhortations on patience. Note the circumstances in which we are to be patient and for what reason.

**a.** Rom. 12:12 _____

**b.** Eph. 4:1–2 _____

**c.** Col. 3:12–14 _____

**d.** 1 Thess. 5:14 _____

**e.** 2 Tim. 4:2 _____

**f.** James 5:7–11 _____

**10.** Do you agree or disagree with the following statements?

    **a.** I can get angry and still be patient. _____

_____

    **b.** Patience is something you just have to grit your teeth and do. _____

_____

Through this study on patience, we see that our God was patient with Israel, even in its stubborn, sinful state. He was patient with his people as would be a loving father. He remained true to them by preserving a remnant, even in their disobedience. Often the Old Testament prophets, along with David in the Psalms, repeat what God spoke of himself in Exodus 34:6: "The LORD, the LORD, the compassionate and gracious God, *slow to anger,* abounding in love and faithfulness. . . . " (emphasis mine). God wants to continually remind us that patience is an integral part of his character.

We also learned that even though we may get impatient waiting on God, God's timetable is different from ours. God does answer, in his time frame, and in his way. He did answer Abraham and David, and he will answer us. At the heart of his timetable is the desire that all people will come to repentance.

The book of Proverbs teaches the importance of patience. We learned that patience can turn the direction of an argument and is significant in our speech.

Lastly, we saw that the New Testament loudly speaks about patience. We are to bear up with one another in patience. We are to rebuke, reprove, and exhort with patience. We are to be patient with everyone. (Sorry, no exceptions here!) And we are to be patient, even in trials.

Yes, God endured man's sinfulness and rebellion, and we, too, can commit ourselves to persevere. We, too, through our unswerving trust in God's character, can bear a crop of patience. Let's see how we can grow these truths into much fruit for him.

## APPLICATIONS

**11.** Take time to reflect on God's patience with you. List those times you have been disobedient and aloof, and thank him for bearing with you. _____

_____

_____

_____

_____

**12.** We usually allow our circumstances to dictate our level of patience. Look at the following circumstances. Which ones eat away at your patience? Remember, God wants to use his Spirit within you to make a difference in how you respond to your daily delights and drudgeries. Allow his Word and Spirit to cleanse you of your bent towards impatience. Remember, you are free to make right choices as you yield yourself to God's Spirit.

| | | |
|---|---|---|
| spilled milk | conflicting opinion | car trouble |
| late bus | irate neighbor | inefficient co-worker |
| lazy teen | pet mess | sick child |
| potty-training child | door salesperson | fighting kids |
| traffic jams | late husband | a cold |
| broken appliance | grocery lines | inconsiderate roomie |
| messy rooms | demanding boss | |

Ask God to reveal an area of your life that you desire the Spirit to work on in the area of patience. Commit this area to God and be accountable to one other Bible study member to bear more of the fruit of patience.

**13.** We also learned that patience involves waiting on God to answer prayer. David and Abraham both waited on God—and God did answer. For what certain event are you currently waiting on God?

a house sale      good health to return
a wanted pregnancy      financial needs to be met
the right job      return of wayward
salvation for a loved one        friend/relative
other. . .

Commit this event to God. Focus on him; rest in him. Remember, in our society of fast-food franchises, microwaved meatloaf, and instant coffee, it's really hard for us to *wait* for anything! Yet, God desires us to be "kingdom women," equipped with a special brand of patience through the enabling of his Spirit.

**MEMORY VERSE**

> The Lord is not slow in keeping his promise, as some understand slowness. He is patient with you, not wanting anyone to perish, but everyone to come to repentance.
>
> 2 Peter 3:9

| GEMS |
| --- |
| |

# 7

## KINDNESS

The Joneses. They were your typical, middle-class family. They had two kids, a boy and a girl, a dog named Spot, and a cat named Silky. Dad worked steadily, Monday through Friday. Mom ran the house and the "family taxi," while the children did above average in school. After school Sonny played soccer, and Sarah practiced piano lessons. Saturdays were reserved for fun, and Sunday mornings you'd always see them sitting in church together. They were your happy all-American family, until . . .

Dad lost his job. The money stopped flowing. Mom made smaller meals. No more piano lessons. Dad and Mom began to fight a lot, so the children hid in their rooms, lost in the world of earphone radios. Dad started sulking. He was downright depressed most of the time.

Dad became abusive—not only verbally, but physically. Mom was stressed out and had little pleasure in the daily routine she once so enjoyed. Distraught, she planned her escape. The children spent less time at home now, and their choice of friends would make any caring parent wince.

No one seemed to care that this family was falling apart. They hurt desperately. Not only did they need material food, but even more so they needed strong counsel on forgiveness and genuine encouragement. Where were their Christian family members when they needed them most?

There *are* many Christian families out there hurting all alone. Many, many Christians lose heart during the hard times in their lives, some never to return to their true faith. Without the loving support of kind actions in their lives, they can slip into depression, and the worries of this world can choke out their love for and commitment to God.

Yes, kind actions provide needed support, and Christians of today have much to learn about implementing kindness. This chapter will teach you about God's divine kindness, and how we as God's vessels can cheer despairing hearts through kind acts. As you study this fifth aspect of the Spirit's fruit, may you be enriched and then overflow with his kindness.

## BACKGROUND

The New Testament Greek word for kindness is *chrēstotēs*. Originally, it carried the idea of usefulness. Connotations of goodness and generosity spring from kindness, and in the Septuagint (the Greek translation of the Old Testament) this word is used more of God than anyone else. Often in the Old Testament it is translated as "good," and it means not only moral excellence, but a quality of heart and emotion.

Kindness is dictated by tenderness and goodness. One who is kind is one who is disposed to do good to others and to make them happy. Kindness is activated by uprightness interwoven with true goodness.

This benevolent kindness characterizes our God. In the

Old Testament, several times God's kindness is translated as *chesed,* a word which deals with loyal love, and kindness. It is only a synonym of the Greek word for kindness, but there is a relationship between the words.

## STUDY QUESTIONS

**1.** Read the following Old Testament verses concerning God's kindness. Who did he show kindness to and how did he manifest it?

| | To Whom | How |
|---|---|---|
| Gen. 32:9–12 | | |
| Gen. 39:20–23 | | |
| Ruth 2:19–20 | | |
| 2 Sam. 22:47–51 | | |
| Isa. 63:7–8 | | |

**2.** Read the following New Testament verses. How did God show his kindness, and what effect does it have on those who accept his kindness?

|  | To Whom | Effects |
|---|---|---|
| Luke 6:35 |  |  |
| Rom. 2:3–4 |  |  |
| Eph. 2:4–7 |  |  |
| Titus 3:3–5 |  |  |
| 1 Peter 2:1–3 (*Chrēstotēs* is translated "good" in NIV here) |  |  |

From the Old Testament we learn that God ruled kindly. He generously displayed his kindness to Jacob in multiplying his material goods. He showed kindness to the unjustly imprisoned Joseph by giving him favor in the sight of the jailer. He showed kindness to Ruth and Naomi by giving Ruth, the widowed foreigner, a generous boss who eventually became her loving husband—and through their lineage came Jesus! At the end of David's life we find him declaring God's kindness as a Rock of deliverance. Also, we learn from Isaiah that God in his kindness became the Savior of Israel.

In the New Testament, we continue to see God showering his kindness. His kindness is impartial—it also pours on the ungrateful and wicked. His kindness brings humanity to repentance. His kindness is rich in grace through Jesus Christ, and it is in his kindness that he saves us and renews us through his Spirit.

Now let's see what we can learn about kindness from David.

**Read 2 Sam. 9:1–7** (Here kindness is the word *chesed*, meaning loyal love. *Elios* is also used, which is the idea of mercy.)

   **3.** Whose kindness did David want to show (v. 3)? _____

   **4.** To whom did David show kindness? _____

   **5.** What did he do to show kindness? _____

_____

This is a remarkable example of kindness. Historically, relatives of the previous king were disposed of. But here, David, because of his great love for Jonathan and respect for God's chosen king, Saul, invites Mephibosheth to share at his table for the remainder of his lifetime. He also restored to Mephibosheth his family's land.

The book of wisdom, Proverbs, also gives some insight on kindness. (Here we see the word *eleeō*, which also means "mercy.")

**Read Prov. 12:25**

   **6.** What power is there in a kind word? _____

_____

**Read Prov. 14:21, 31**

   **7.** To whom is a blessed person kind? _____

_____

**8.** How can you honor God? _____

_____

**9.** How can you show contempt for God? _____

_____

**10.** What is a practical way to be kind to the needy? _____

_____

We find *chrēstos,* the adjective for *chrēstotēs,* in the New Testament in Matt. 11:28–30. Jesus is talking about his yoke. In v. 30 he says "For my yoke is *chrēstos* [easy] and my burden is light." Here *chrēstos* can mean well-fitting. In other words, service for Christ is not ruthlessly imposed upon us; no, it is a kindly service, tailor-made by our Lord for us to do.

**Read Eph. 4:32**

**11.** What is one result of being a kind and compassionate person? _____

_____

**12.** Who set the example of forgiving others, and how does not following his example affect your level of kindness? _____

_____

_____

**Read 1 Cor. 15:33** (*chrēstotēs* here is translated as "good" in NIV)

**13.** How does bad company affect the quality of kindness in your life? _____

_____

**14.** Why do you think this is true? _____

_____

_____

## APPLICATIONS

Through God's Spirit we learn how to be kind. Our kindness cannot be selective as God's is not biased. Our kindness must be forgiving and generous.

**15.** Think about God's kindness for a few minutes. Note how God's kindness has reached down to you. Praise him for his kindness and for putting a kind spirit within you. _____

_____

**16.** Ask God to reveal any person that you are currently not forgiving. Meditate on Eph. 4:32. Plan your method of attack on how you are going to forgive that person. If you have problems doing this, reflect on how much God has forgiven you through Christ. Let his kindness motivate you to obedience. _____

_____

_____

**17.** Evaluate your friends and the activities you schedule. Are they influencing you to be kind? Remember, Scripture warns us that bad company affects our kindly attitudes. (There certainly must be a proper balance here, as God does want us to be salt and light on this earth. Just take a few moments to evaluate your peers, your forms of entertainment, etc., to see if you are more influenced by kindly or unkindly activities.) What have you discovered? _____

_____

_____

**18.** To stimulate you towards specific ways you can show kindness, in the chart below, match up the kind actions with specific people. Some actions match up with more than one person.

| Person | What to Give |
|---|---|
| a rest home patient | a cheerful word |
| a wife-beater | a bag of groceries |
| a neglected child | forgiveness |
| a family without income | a friendly, drop-in visit |
| a person in unbelief | a toy or clothes, read a story |
| a disabled person | tell them of God's kindness |
| a depressed person | a helping hand in doing chores |

Let these motivate you to think of someone you can show kindness to this week. Remember, God has equipped us with his Spirit so that we can bear a bountiful harvest for his glory. Ask God to help you be more kind.

## MEMORY VERSE

But when the kindness and love of God our Savior appeared, he saved us, not because of righteous things we had done, but because of his mercy. He saved us through the washing of rebirth and renewal by the Holy Spirit.

Titus 3:4–5

**GEMS**

# 8

## GOODNESS

---

What do you think of when you hear the word *goodness?* Often we hear this word, or its adjective, "good"—"Goodie-two-shoes," "Goodness gracious," "Have you been a good girl today?," "Surely goodness shall follow me," "She's good-looking," "She's good-natured." But what does it mean?

*Good* is one of the most common words in English, but in order to define it we must have a concrete foundation to build upon. Today *good* seems to mean "average" because, compared with the superlatives *super, great,* and *fantastic, good* seems kind of ordinary. How does the dictionary define it?

*Webster's* dictionary has many definitions for "good." They include: "of a favorable character or tendency; bountiful, fertile; handsome, attractive; agreeable, pleasant; virtuous, just, commendable, loyal; a praiseworthy character."

What about in ancient days? What did *goodness* mean for ancient non-Christians? Some saw good as the experience of pleasure and the eradication of pain. Others sought knowledge to fill the cup of goodness. Although they have some redeeming benefits, all of these simplified philosophies can lead to danger—to a path of evil.

So, for the Christian, what is goodness? God is goodness. He is our foundational standard of goodness, and the revelation of his Word tells us how to live it. Are you good according to God's standards or according to some shifting societal standards? As we study this sixth aspect of God's spiritual fruit, may you be spurred on to more goodness—God's way.

## BACKGROUND

In Gal. 5:22 this quality is represented by the Greek word *agathosunē*. It is only mentioned in three other places in the New Testament. *Agathosunē* is a quality of conduct and action which is closely tied to generosity—God's generosity. *Agathosunē* stresses moral judgment, with a zeal for goodness and truth in rebuking. It is tied to *chrestotes* (kindness) because the generosity which springs from the heart is that which is kind.

*Agathosunē* is also connected with the word *dikaiosunē*, which means justice. In Eph. 5:9, justice (righteousness) and truth are linked with goodness. Justice is a quality which gives a woman what is her due; goodness is the quality which exceeds that, for it desires to give a woman all that is helpful to her, and to her benefit. In other words, the person who is *just* sticks to the letter of his contract; the person who is *good* goes beyond the fine print.

Although the adjective for goodness, *agathos*, is used over 100 times in the New Testament, *agathosunē* is rarely used. It is therefore helpful to look at both *agathosunē* and *agathos* in the Septuagint* (the Greek translation of the Old Testament). Let's begin by discovering how God is goodness.

## STUDY QUESTIONS

**1.** Read the following verses and note those that speak specifically of God's goodness. Also write down what actions show this quality.

|  | Verses | Actions |
|---|---|---|
| Exod. 33:17–20 |  |  |
| 1 Chron. 16:1, 7, 23–36 |  |  |
| 2 Chron. 5:1–3, 11–14 |  |  |
| Neh. 9:1–35 |  |  |
| Ps. 118:1, 29 |  |  |

## Read Rom. 12:1–2

**2.** What kind of will does God possess? _____

---

*The Septuagint is a Greek translation of the Hebrew Old Testament and was written before Christ's day.

**3.** How can we know God's good will? _____

_____

### Read 2 Thess. 1:11-12

**4.** For what did Paul, Silas, and Timothy pray for the Thessalonians? _____

_____

**5.** Who could enable the Thessalonians to complete good acts? _____

_____

**6.** What is the result of "good" actions? _____

_____

### Read 2 Tim. 3:16-17

**7.** How can we be equipped for every good work? _____

_____

### Read Titus 2:3-5

**8.** Whose responsibility is it to see that the young mothers know what is good? _____

_____

**9.** Do you see this teaching team developed in your church? _____

_____

**10.** What is the result of teaching what is good to the younger women? _____

_____

**Read Eph. 2:8–10**

   **11.** How have we been saved? _____

_____

   **12.** What have we been saved to do? _____

_____

   **13.** In whom are we capable of doing good works? _____

_____

**Read 2 Thess. 2:16–17**

   **14.** Who will encourage and strengthen you in good deeds and words? _____

_____

   **15.** When you feel like doing something evil, who can you turn to for eternal encouragement and good hope? _____

_____

**Read Heb. 10:22–25**

   **16.** What actions are we to spur on in one another?

   **17.** Who gives us the ability to spur one another on to love and good deeds? _____

_____

   **18.** How does having a clean conscience and maintaining a clear perspective of the hope that is in us relate to stimulating one another to love and good deeds? _____

_____

**Read Heb. 13:15–16**

   **19.** Through whom can we offer God a sacrifice of praise?

_____

**20.** How do you think praising God and sharing with others relates to doing good? _____

_____

### Read 1 Peter 2:11–12

**21.** What must we abstain from in order to live good lives?

_____

**22.** What is an end result of living a good life? _____

_____

### Read 2 Peter 1:3–9

**23.** Out of what character quality did God call us? _____

_____

**24.** How has he equipped us for "godliness"? _____

_____

**25. a.** What are the seven things to be added to our faith?

_____

_____

  **b.** Which is listed first? _____

_____

**26. a.** If you possess these qualities, what will happen?

_____

  **b.** If you don't have them what have you forgotten? _____

_____

What have we learned from this chapter on goodness? First of all, we learned that God displayed his glory and goodness to Moses. He also showered his goodness on the Israelites by giving them fertile land and victorious strength in battle. He gave of his goodness through his faithful love to an often disobedient people. Today he shows his goodness by calling us to himself and again *giving* of himself. Through his divine power he gives us everything that we need for life and godliness (2 Peter 1:3).

We saw the importance of the Word, and how it equips us to do good works. The transforming of our minds allows us to approve God's perfect, good will. We are God's workmanship, created for good works.

Lastly, we learned the role each of us must take in spurring each other to do good works. The older women must teach the younger that which is good. We might have good works as the trademark of our lives, because good works result in bringing new members into the family of God. Yes, good works should be our trademark, but they should never be confused with our ticket into heaven—as the cults would have us believe.

## APPLICATIONS

**27.** Take a moment and reflect on God's goodness. How has he been good to you? List one specific way you have partaken of God's goodness. _____

_____

**28.** Evaluate your time in the Word. Are you in the Word daily? On a scale of one to ten (one being a non-meditating sluggard, and ten a super-reading saint) where are you regarding your time in the Word? Remember, 2 Tim. 3:16–17 tells us that through the useful teaching, rebuking, correcting, and training of the Word we become equipped for every good work. Are you allowing the Word to transform your thinking so that you will be able to approve God's good will? _____

**29.** When was the last time you brought praise to God by doing a good work? Maybe you led a person to Christ by first doing good works for them, or perhaps you yourself became interested in spiritual dimensions because of someone else's good works. Write down one situation below, and relate it to the group, thus spurring each other on to more good works. Good works must diligently be sown not for our salvation, but for an abundant harvest of praise to our God.

_____

_____

_____

_____

**30.** If your local body of believers has not implemented the scriptural steps for teaching young mothers, as found in Titus 2:3–5, take the initial steps to do so. Let's face it, enough family life is disintegrating without the church ignoring the proper steps for teaching young women. We must take our Bible seriously, and follow scriptural principles. Write down five principles of your own that you feel come under the heading, "to teach what is good."

**a.** _____

**b.** _____

**c.** _____

**d.** _____

**e.** _____

**31.** List one specific person you are going to stimulate to love and to good deeds. How are you going to do it? _____

_____

_____

## MEMORY VERSES

Give thanks to the LORD, for he is good; his love endures forever.

Ps. 118:1

In the same way, let your light shine before men, that they may see your good deeds and praise your Father in heaven.

Matt. 5:16

**GEMS**

# 9

## FAITHFULNESS

Faithfulness. Does such a character trait exist today? Often we hear of marriages ruptured by unfaithfulness. Businesses dissolve under the pressure of a disloyal partner. Family relationships disintegrate in the midst of broken promises.

The Christian community is not immune; the lack of faithfulness permeates even *our* world. In a world where there is so much unfaithfulness, how can we, as God's women, be faithful?

As you study this seventh aspect of God's spiritual fruit, allow God to teach you by his example. Let his character of faithfulness instill in you the ability to be faithful. May you truly become faithful in new areas of growth as you are empowered by his Spirit.

### BACKGROUND

The New Testament Greek word for faithfulness is *pistis*. It conveys the quality of reliability, trustworthiness, and loyalty.

*Pistis* speaks of a person utterly reliable, filled with integrity, fidelity, and dependability.

Often *pistis* is translated "faith" in the New Testament. This faith is normally the doctrinal statement of personal belief in the Lord Jesus Christ for salvation. The same word, when speaking of the fruit of the Spirit, is used to identify a life-quality of faithfulness in one who is a believer.

Some of the Greek synonyms relating to faithfulness are "solemn promise, troth, oath, proof, pledge, trust, confidence, faith, and belief." Galatians 5:22 uses *faithfulness* to represent this concept.

It boils down to this: a faithful woman is someone that you know is going to keep her word; if she tells you she will do something, it's done! You can bet your life on the faithful person's word.

Let's study the Scriptures and see what a faithful God we have.

## STUDY QUESTIONS

**1.** Read the following Old Testament verses and discover how God has been faithful in history. Note to whom and in what way God was faithful.

| | To Whom | How |
|---|---|---|
| Gen. 32:9–12 | | |
| Exod. 34:4–8 | | |
| Deut. 31:30–<br>32:4 | | |

|  | To Whom | How |
|---|---|---|
| Neh. 9:1, 32–35 | | |
| Ps. 33:4 | | |
| Ps. 57:1–3 | | |
| Isa. 25:1 | | |
| Isa. 61:8–9 | | |
| Lam. 3:19–24 | | |

**2.** Now read the following New Testament verses and state the specific way God is faithful.

**a.** 1 Cor. 1:4–9 _____

_____

**b.** 1 Cor. 10:13 _____

_____

**c.** 1 Thess. 5:23–24 _____

_____

**d.** 2 Thess. 3:3 _____

_____

**e.** Heb. 10:23 _____

_____

**f.** 1 Peter 4:19 _____

_____

**g.** 1 John 1:9 _____

_____

**h.** Rev. 1:5 _____

_____

**3.** Let's look at Ps. 89. Find all the verses that speak of God's faithfulness. Read it slowly; soak up the truths of this psalm. _____

_____

_____

_____

What have we learned about God's faithfulness? First of all, God is faithful to keep his promises. We see this continually throughout Jewish history. Jacob, Moses, Nehemiah, David, Isaiah, Jeremiah, Paul, Peter, and John all state the truth: God is faithful. He is a solid rock, he is firm, reliable, available, and accessible to his children. He lovingly provides a "way of escape" in temptation. God faithfully strengthens and protects us from the evil one. He also faithfully forgives.

We have learned about God's faithfulness; now let's look at what human faithfulness (trustworthiness) involves.

**Read Josh. 24:14–15**

**4.** When Joshua assembled the Israelites, how did he request them to show faithfulness to God? _____

_____

**5.** Are there any "gods" or idols in your life that you must throw away in order to serve God more faithfully? _____

_____

**Read Luke 16:10–13**

**6.** What area of faithfulness is being addressed? _____

_____

**7.** How do trustworthiness and faithfulness relate to each other? _____

_____

**Read 1 Cor. 4:1–5**

**8.** In this passage who must be faithful? _____

_____

**9.** How are they to be faithful? _____

_____

**Read 1 Tim. 3:11**

**10.** Who is to be faithful (trustworthy)? _____

_____

**11.** What is linked with trustworthiness? _____

_____

**12.** How do malicious talking, respect, and temperance relate to faithfulness? _____

_____

_____

**Read 1 Peter 4:10**

**13.** What area of faithfulness is addressed? _____

_____

**14.** How do faithfulness and serving others relate? _____

_____

Let's recap our discoveries. Faithfulness to God involves putting aside other gods. We must be faithful to God with our talents and material goods. Those entrusted with the truth must be faithful, their motives pure. Deacons' wives must put malicious talk aside, and be temperate and trustworthy in everything. In addition, we must serve faithfully with our spiritual gifts.

### APPLICATIONS

**15.** Reflect on the truth of God's faithfulness. Recall the various Scripture passages which tell of God's faithfulness. Take time to talk with God, to praise him for his faithfulness. Write below some of the ways God has been faithful to you, and share these specifics with the group. _____

_____

_____

**16.** How do each of the women in the following situations lack faithfulness, and what could they do differently next time to display the fruit of faithfulness?

**a.** Carol's schedule has been very busy lately, and she notices that her young son is whining a lot. She tells him that in thirty minutes they will piece together a puzzle. The phone rings in twenty-nine minutes. It's a "ministry" call, a friend who is going through deep trouble. Carol's on the phone for forty-five minutes. When she hangs up the phone, her son is nowhere to be found. _____

_____

_____

_____

**b.** Rachel's neighbor, who is not a Christian yet, is having a Tupperware party. Rachel tells her that she'll be there, and then forgets about it. Rachel sees the neighbor in her garden the next day, but doesn't know what to say. _____

_____

_____

_____

**c.** A special friend confides in Julie. She tells Julie some very personal struggles she's currently battling. Julie decides to tell her husband and another "prayer" partner about it, without the friend's permission. Soon a whole circle of friends knows of her struggles. _____

_____

_____

_____

**d.** Sonja's an avid romance novel reader. She finds that the scenes she reads about linger in her mind long after she has put the book down. In fact, she's beginning to fantasize about some of the characters in the novel. _____

_____

_____

_____

**e.** Jesus Christ is definitely Sandy's Lord. She has a weekly Bible study in her home. The desire for a comfortable and appealing environment for the study compelled Sandy to go out and buy a more suitable living room couch and chair set. The payments are kind of high, but she realizes that in just six short months she'll be able to resume giving to her local church. _____

_____

_____

_____

**f.** Connie's known for some time that her spiritual gift is "helping." In the past, she has served joyfully in many "helping" ways, but now she's tired of serving with no recognition. In fact, Connie's currently just sitting on the sidelines because she's decided it's about time someone else served. _____

_____

_____

_____

**17.** From the following list, select one area in which you need to grow more faithfulness. Commit this area to God, and specifically ask God's Spirit to enable you to be more faithful in that area.

　　my tongue _____

　　my talents _____

　　my time _____

my spiritual gifts _____

my material goods _____

my marriage _____

my employer _____

my family _____

my relationship to my church body and its leaders

_____

other _____

## MEMORY VERSE

He is the Rock, his works are perfect, and all his ways
are just. A faithful God who does no wrong, upright and
just is he.

Deut. 32:4

| GEMS |
|------|
|      |
|      |
|      |
|      |
|      |
|      |

# 10

## GENTLENESS

Oh, yuck! The baby has thrown up again, decorating me with curdled milk, complete with tidbits of cereal topped with bananas. That was the third time this morning, and the fragrance of soured milk is getting a little old. The flu bug is no fun. Especially when you have nine in the family, and it's making its vicious rounds.

As I wipe out David's ears and rinse off the residue from his dark curly hair, I find that my motions are a little harsh. I just want to get the mess cleaned up, and get prepared for the next wave of whatever.

In the kitchen, Kevin has the music box going. The radio is blaring, muffling out his deep cough. Thank goodness the flu hasn't affected his digestive tract yet, but all the extra noise of having him and the other kids home sick has me more than a little bit edgy. I find myself barking at the children to get back in bed in a tone I'm certainly not proud of. And what quality of the Spirit am I studying this week? Oh, yes, gentleness. Gentleness even in caring for the sick . . . or maybe it's dealing with a stubborn co-worker . . . or maybe it's making decisions for an aged, senile parent.

Lord, help us! As we study the eighth aspect of your Spirit's fruit, grant us knowledge to see you clearly. Plant your character of gracious gentleness deep into our hearts.

## BACKGROUND

In Gal. 5:23 we see the Greek word *praütēs* translated "gentleness." In secular Greek writing it was used to refer to an ointment which soothed the pain of an ulcerous wound. It was also used to describe the vocal tone of a lover. Plato, in *The Laws,* used it when writing of a child asking a doctor to treat him in the gentlest possible manner.

In the Old Testament the words "poor," "abased," and "humble" are some of the synonyms for gentleness. This is so because of economic conditions during Old Testament times, but the synonyms for gentleness are also appropriate to convey the attitude of being poor before God.

Our Rabbi Jesus best summarized it by saying, "Blessed are the poor in spirit" (Matt. 5:3), by which he meant that one must come to God with empty hands. Two verses later, he expressed a similar idea when he said "Blessed are the meek [or 'gentle'] for they will inherit the earth." The person who is "poor in spirit" comes to God with empty hands, and then two verses later leaves with a deed to heavenly acres!

We will discover that the word *praütēs* is used of two great biblical characters: Moses and Jesus. We will find that gentleness is the opposite of arrogance, bitterness, wildness, or pride. It has to do with lowliness and humility in which there is no arrogance and only delight to serve. It has been said that gentle is the person who is always angry at the right thing and never angry at the wrong thing.

## STUDY QUESTIONS

Read the following verses describing Christ.

Zech. 9:9 (See Matt. 21:4–7 for the fulfillment)
Matt. 11:28–30
2 Cor. 10:1

**1.** What quality is listed in all of these verses? _____

_____

**2.** Think of the various difficult situations Christ dealt with (such as throwing the money changers out of the temple, dealing with the Pharisees, and working many miracles). How does knowing that Christ's character was described as being gentle give you a new awareness of what true gentleness means? _____

_____

_____

**3.** Does gentleness equal "pansiness"? _____

_____

**Read Num. 12:3** (*Praütēs* is translated "very humble" here.)

**4. a.** Who is described as gentle (very humble)? _____

_____

**b.** Relate to one another the various tasks God called Moses to do. Was he a "wimp"? _____

_____

_____

It is important to realize that gentleness is not a wimpy, weak characteristic, but a very controlled, positive strength that God desires to grow in our lives. A gentle life is one tamed by God's Spirit, one which defuses dissensions and cools hot tempers. Its strong mortar builds healthy relationships, nurturing the fainthearted with quiet, caring morsels of love. In the following verses we will see when Christians are called especially to display this fruit.

**5.** Read the following. List the who, when, and what or how Christians are to be regarding gentleness. (Each Scripture passage may not clearly state all the answers, but fill in as many as you can find.)

|  | Who | When | What or How |
|---|---|---|---|
| Gal. 6:1 | | | |
| Eph. 4:1–3 | | | |
| Phil. 4:4–5 | | | |
| 1 Thess. 2:7–9 | | | |
| 1 Tim. 6:11–12 | | | |
| 2 Tim. 2:22–26 | | | |

|  | **Who** | **When** | **What or How** |
|---|---|---|---|
| Titus 3:1–2 |  |  |  |
| James 1:19–21 |  |  |  |
| James 3:13 |  |  |  |
| 1 Peter 3:15–16 |  |  |  |

**6.** Which verses talk about witnessing? _____

**7.** Which verses talk about correcting a family member?

_____

**8.** Which verses talk about humbling ourselves before God's Word? _____

The last Scripture passage we will look at is very crucial for women.

### Read 1 Peter 3:1–6, then zero in on 3:3–4

**9.** What does God consider to be "unfading beauty"? _____

_____

**10.** How does one cultivate a "gentle and quiet spirit"? ___

_____

From this study we have learned that our biblical examples of gentleness are Jesus and Moses. Even though in the English language we may conjure up some "Melvin Milktoast" image for someone who is gentle, we realize that gentleness is a strong quality. Through its quiet gracefulness, it fosters healthy relationships and brings rest to the weary and harmony to the hostile person.

As believers, we are admonished to be gentle in witnessing, gentle in correcting, gentle in our relationship with our mates, and gentle in teaching.

## APPLICATIONS

**11.** Take time to reflect on Christ's gentleness. Praise him for his gentle ways.

**12.** Grade yourself on a scale of one to ten (one meaning you are uncontrollably explosive, and ten meaning you have harnessed your strength) on any of the following situations you may have encountered this week. If you experienced none of these, write your own situation in the space marked "other."

Dealing with a picky neighbor _____

Correcting a child _____

Responding to husband _____

Teaching your Sunday school class _____

Answering an irate phone call _____

Defending your faith _____

Confronting a teenager _____

Working with a difficult co-worker _____

Other _____

**13.** Note whether you agree or disagree with the following statements, and explain why:

**a.** A gentle person never speaks out of turn. _____

_____

**b.** A gentle person does not make a good military sergeant. _____

_____

**14.** Think about the important passage of 1 Peter 3:3–4, and take some time to evaluate where your priorities are. Do you spend more time cultivating outward beauty than inward beauty? Perhaps you would be challenged by an idea Linda Weber, one of the pastors' wives at Good Shepherd Community Church, suggested to our group. She suggested taking a blank calendar and every day that you spend quality time in the Word, leave the space blank. Every day that you do not spend time in the Word, cross it off. After a month, evaluate what percentage of the month you were actually spending time with God. If you missed a few days it may not seem like much, but if you look at the whole year on the basis of how you did that month, you may discover that there are many days when you didn't seek God.

## MEMORY VERSE

Come to me, all you who are weary and burdened, and I will give you rest. Take my yoke upon you and learn from me, for I am gentle and humble in heart, and you will find rest for your souls . . .

Matt. 11:28–29

| GEMS |
| --- |
|  |

# 11

## SELF-CONTROL

It started so innocently. Just a longing glance at a friend from yesteryear. A friendly hello and a comfortable conversation led to a simple lunch of reminiscing about the "good ol' days." Now Sally found herself trapped and drowning in an adulterous relationship. Somewhere she had gone adrift. So subtly, yet swiftly, her sin sank her into despair. Her so-called momentary pleasure will leave Sally "shipwrecked" with scars for a long time to come.

What had Sally forgotten? Why did she succumb to what she knew was absolutely wrong? Where was her self-control when she needed it?

Our ever-evolving free-sex society needs self-control. The "Me Generation" says, "Go for it and don't look back. You deserve a little excitement, a little fling." It continues to lie by saying that there's no need to be prudish anymore—there are plenty of reliable birth control methods on the market.

Besides, you don't have to assume any responsibility for your actions—if you become pregnant just abort the unwanted baby.

Lies, lies, lies!

The Bible speaks the truth. It clearly addresses the issue of self-control and the ensnaring repercussions for those who live without it.

Why must we be self-controlled? Because God created us with many appetites for pleasure. Our sexuality is certainly one of them. He also provided us with a guidebook, the Bible, to teach us how to deal with our desires. Sex is beautifully designed by the Master Creator, and is fulfilling in the right context—marriage. It is ugly, however, outside the security of biblical guidelines, and its drive is powerful, causing many a heartbreak for those who ignore its wisdom.

Don't let your "garden plot" become a garbage dump soiled by worldly values. Rather, let God's Spirit do a cooperative work within you, keeping you alert and cleansed. Let his Spirit empower you to say yes to him. As you study self-control, may you gain a clearer understanding of how to bear this fruit in your daily life.

## BACKGROUND

The last of the nine characteristics of the fruit of the Spirit is self-control. Although the particular word in Greek, *egkrateia*, refers to self-control in the area of sexuality, we will be looking at other areas in our lives that will be enhanced by the fruit of self-control. We will be looking at a life that is disciplined, mastered, strengthened, and empowered by the Spirit. It is a life that can, and does, say no! to the world. It is a life that is lived in the world, yet remains unstained by the world.

Aside from the Galatians passage, *egkrateia* is only mentioned two other times in the New Testament. Its corresponding verb, *egkrateuomai,* occurs two times. It is defined as "self-controlled" or "to exercise self-control." The corresponding adjective, *egkratēs,* occurs only once in the New Testament. *Egkratēs* is used in relation to elders being self-controlled, sober, just, and holy.

In the New Testament, self-control relates to abstaining from evil in general, and sexual restraint in particular.

There are many New Testament words which are translated as "self-control." Don't think that every time you see a verse reference that it is using the word *egkrateia.* Since it is used a limited number of times, however, looking at the Septuagint will help us see which times the meaning of *egkrateia* is intended in the Old Testament.

## STUDY QUESTIONS

**1.** Read the following Old Testament verses that have the idea of self-control. Note who showed self-control and in what context. What emotion did each have under control?

**a.** Gen. 43:26–32 _____

_____

**b.** Esther 5:5–10 (restrained) _____

_____

Although self-control in the New Testament often deals with the sexual aspects of life, it can be applied to life in general. The apostolic fathers, the first group of Christian writers other than the New Testament writers, wrote of self-control in the late years of the first century and in the first half of the second century. In fact, they wrote a great deal about the self-controlled life.

Clement of Rome wrote that self-control was a gift of God, and one of the greatest gifts! Clement claimed self-control to be part of the very basis of the Christian life. He wrote, "How blessed and wonderful are God's gifts . . . self-control with sanctification.'' Polycarp specifically addressed Christian women to tenderly love their husbands, and to love all others in chastity (self-control). Secular writings of the period are not helpful on this subject, though some scholars try to compare self-control with the lists of virtues in pagan Greek philosophy. There are, however, no meaningful comparisons.

We should not falsify the doctrine of self-control by avoiding every pleasure in the world and calling it ''evil,'' for God called all of his creation ''good.'' Rather, the doctrine of self-control puts everything under Christ's subjection. Yes, self-control equals Christ-control.

**Read Phil. 3:20–21**

**2.** Who has the power to bring everything under his control? _____

_____

**3.** Where is the Christian's citizenship? _____

_____

**4.** Who will transform our lowly bodies to conform to Christ's? _____

_____

**5.** How does knowing these truths make you want to live a life that pleases and submits to the all-powerful Christ—to live a life controlled by the very Spirit of Christ? _____

_____

_____

**6.** Let's examine the book of Proverbs. Read the following verses and note what they say about self-control or the lack of it, and in what area.

**a.** Prov. 12:18 (reckless words are ones spoken rashly, without control) _____

_____

**b.** Prov. 23:19–21 _____

_____

**c.** Prov. 25:16 _____

_____

**d.** Prov. 25:28 _____

_____

**e.** Prov. 29:11 _____

_____

Read the following exhortations on being self-controlled or temperate.

**Read Rom. 8:6–9**

**7.** What two minds are battling? _____

_____

**8.** What is the result of each kind of mind? _____

_____

**9. a.** As a Christian, who are we equipped with to live a life under control? _____

_____

**b.** How does submission relate to self-control, and to whom must the Christian submit? _____

_____

**Read 1 Cor. 7:8–9**

**10.** Who is Paul addressing? _____

_____

**11.** What area is addressed and what is the solution given?

_____

**Read 1 Thess. 4:3–4**

**12.** What does God's will call us to be? _____

_____

**13.** What should we avoid? _____

_____

**14.** How does having a mindset towards holiness (separateness from the world) help a Christian to control her own body? _____

_____

**Read 1 Thess. 5:4–8**

**15. a.** During great persecution, what does Paul admonish the Thessalonians to be? _____

_____

**b.** How does being "alert" affect your self-control (v. 6)? _____

_____

**16.** Contrast day and night. Which do Christians belong to and why? _____

_____

**17.** What three things are we to put on, and how will they help us in our battle for self-control? _____

_____

### Read Titus 2:3–5, 11–14

**18.** What are the older women to teach the younger women? _____

_____

**19.** How does self-control relate to being pure, kind, busy at home, and subject to one's husband? _____

_____

**20. a.** What does God's gracious salvation teach us? _____

**b.** If we are living a life lacking in self-control, what might we have forgotten? _____

_____

_____

### Read 1 Peter 1:13–16

**21. a.** What must we do in order to be self-controlled? ____

_____

**b.** With what hope are we to prepare our minds? _____

_____

**22. a.** To whom are we to conform our lives? _____

_____

**b.** What aren't we to conform to? _____

_____

### Read 1 Peter 4:7, 5:8

**23.** What will enhance your prayer life? _____

_____

**24.** How do you think being clearminded and alert relate to being self-controlled? _____

_____

What have we learned about self-control? First of all, to be self-controlled means to submit to the one who has everything under his control. We must be self-controlled in many areas: our tongues, our temper, our eating habits, our sexual appetites, and other pleasures.

There is a battle going on between our flesh and our spirit and we must be alert, clearminded, and prepared for action if we are to be victorious. We must conform our lives to God's holiness and never forget his gracious salvation nor the hope that we have in him. We must remember to say no! to everything that makes us stray from God's holy will for our lives. We also must remember that even though sometimes it is hard to deny fulfilling our wrong desires, the end result is true life and peace.

### APPLICATIONS

**25.** Take time to reflect on God's holiness. Remember how Jesus denied his fleshly desires at the temptation. Praise God for his righteous control over all. Remember that as you submit to God you have this very power within you to make right choices.

**26.** Look over the following areas. Evaluate your life, and choose one particular area where you need more self-control. Pray that God's Spirit will train you to submit even this area to Christ's holiness, and thus bear spiritual fruit.

| | |
|---|---|
| gossiping | eating |
| drinking | spending money |
| exercising | arguing (temper) |
| pill-popping | TV watching |
| working | sleeping |
| dressing sexily | flirting |
| reading romance novels | fantasizing and daydreaming |
| other | |

**27.** Read over and think about the following situations. How do you respond?

**a.** Sears is having its yearly sale and you are dying to go to it, even though last month's Visa charge card is already $200 over budget. Will you be self-controlled? _____

_____

**b.** Do you ever dress a certain way or walk a certain way to get men's attention, even though you may already be married? Does your husband's lack of affection, your own insecurities or your unsatisfying marriage undermine your self-control in your sexual thoughts? _____

_____

_____

**c.** When you go to potluck dinners do you put your whole attention on satisfying your appetite? Do you find that you focus on eating—stuffing yourself to the point of bursting—without having one meaningful conversation? Do you find that over the years you have continually tried to satisfy an inner hunger by eating, so that now you are overweight? (Some people have a medical reason that causes obesity. This question is not directed at such people, but at those who choose to overeat. Overeating is a much condoned sin in the Christian community, but, nevertheless, a harmful one that does not display the fruit of the Spirit.) \_\_\_\_\_

_____

_____

**d.** During social times with business associates, do you find yourself drinking too much? Perhaps you try to calm your nerves or be one of the crowd, only to find yourself tipsy by the end of the meeting. If you drink too much in such situations, are you showing dependence on the Spirit or on the flesh? If you depend on the flesh, do you do so only to discover that you are way out of control? _____

_____

_____

**e.** Do you work a high-pressure job? Do you release stress through a healthy exercise program, good balanced diet, and by focusing on God's perspective of life? Or do you pop pills, yell at your children when you return home, go on shopping sprees, and eat junk food? _____

_____

_____

Hopefully, pondering these life situations will stimulate you to a greater dependence on God's Spirit. Submitting to him will bring a fruitful harvest, and a dimension of true holiness and peace to your life, a life characterized by self-control.

## MEMORY VERSE

Therefore, prepare your minds for action and be self-controlled; set your hope fully on the grace to be given you when Jesus Christ is revealed.

1 Peter 1:13

| GEMS |
|------|
|      |

# 12

## A WELL-WATERED GARDEN

I was outside weeding in the fresh air today. The sun shone brightly on my shoulders as I sat crouched on the grass. Funny thing, the lawn, mowed only a week ago, already looked scraggly, while in the just weeded flowerbed I saw weed roots popping their thorns through the sod. Will we never be done with weeding?

The garden weeds are as tenacious as the "spiritual weeds" in my life. Over the past many months, through the study on the fruit of the Spirit, I have taken in so much of the beauty of our almighty God. My spiritual life has grown rapidly, like a well-watered spring lawn, and I have seen similar growth in sisters' lives. Yet, too, I have seen the weeds of our fallen nature grow—weeds of conceit, envy, and provoking among the family (Gal. 5:26)—and they choke out the bloom, the fruit we desire to grow.

Therefore, in the last study in this workshop on the fruit of the Spirit, let's dig in to the Word. By nourishing ourselves with God's words, we can leave this study with the fresh knowledge planted deep within that our God is indeed a God of love, joy, peace, patience, kindness, goodness, faithfulness, gentleness, and self-control. We will both better know him who we seek, and discover what he is like. Let's constantly focus on the reality that God is here, seeking to empower our lives with his Spirit. By allowing God to dominate our beings, we will become beautiful gardens flourishing with his character.

Also in this study, we will test our knowledge by matching up definitions and fruit. How much did you learn about each quality? (This is for your growth and enjoyment, so don't get too anxious about having all the right answers!)

There's also an opportunity to evaluate. Take time to look over this rich garden of study and see if your life is bearing the knowledge you planted. Share with one another an area you've seen God weed, fertilize, and Son-ripen during this study. He *is* the Master Gardener, and it is his Spirit that works the soil of your heart as you yield to his hand.

## STUDY QUESTIONS

**1.** List by heart the nine qualities of the fruit of the Spirit.

_____

_____

_____

_____

**2.** Write out these verses you've committed to memory.

**a.** Gal. 5:22–23 _____

_____

_____

**b.** Ps. 86:15 _____

_____

_____

**c.** 1 John 4:10 _____

_____

_____

**d.** Phil. 4:4 _____

_____

_____

**e.** Phil. 4:6–7 _____

_____

_____

**f.** 2 Peter 3:9 _____

_____

_____

**g.** Titus 3:4–5 _____

_____

_____

**h.** Ps. 118:1 _____

_____

_____

**i.** Matt. 5:16 _____

_____

_____

**j.** Deut. 32:4 _____

_____

_____

**k.** Matt. 11:28–29 _____

_____

_____

**l.** 1 Peter 1:13 _____

_____

_____

**3.** Note which fruit is defined in each case below.

**a.** *makrothumia*—long-suffering; putting anger afar. ____

_____

**b.** *pistis*—quality of reliability, trustworthiness, and loyalty. _____

_____

**c.** *chrēstotēs*—a quality of the heart and emotion from which goodness springs forth. _____

_____

**d.** *egkrateia*—a life that is disciplined by the Spirit so that it can and does say "no" to the world, especially in the area of sexuality. _____

_____

**e.** *chara*—to rejoice; the inward gladness of heart that comes from knowing and experiencing the presence and perspective of God. _____

_____

**f.** *praütēs*—lowliness and humility in which there is no arrogance, but only delight to serve. _____

_____

**g.** *agathosunē*—quality of conduct and action that is closely tied with God's generosity. _____

_____

**h.** *agapē*—the highest form of love that is active, unconditional, sacrificial, and that seeks only the best for another. _____

_____

**i.** *eirēnē*—the God-given ability to develop and maintain right relationships—not detachments—in every sphere of life. _____

_____

**4.** Read the following verses and list which fruit is addressed. Also, in order to think practically about bearing the fruit, write a way in which *you* can bear this fruit.

**a.** Gal. 6:1 _____

_____

**b.** John 3:16 _____

_____

**c.** 1 John 1:9 _____

_____

**d.** 1 Peter 2:11–12 _____

_____

**e.** Rom. 5:1–2 _____

_____

**f.** Ps. 43:4 _____

_____

**g.** 1 Cor. 10:13 _____

_____

**h.** Rom. 2:3–4 _____

_____

**i.** Eph. 2:10 _____

_____

**j.** 2 Peter 3:9, 15 _____

_____

**k.** 1 Peter 4:7 _____

_____

**l.** 1 John 4:7–21 _____

_____

**m.** Eph. 4:32 _____

_____

**n.** Isa. 26:1–4 _____

_____

**o.** 2 Tim. 4:2 _____

_____

**p.** 1 Peter 3:3–4 _____

_____

**q.** 1 Thess. 4:3–4 _____

_____

**r.** 3 John 4 _____

_____

**5.** In which area of the fruit of the Spirit have you experienced the most blooms these past twelve weeks? Share this experience with the group. _____

_____

_____

## MEMORY VERSE

> The Lord will guide you always; he will satisfy your needs in a sun-scorched land and will strengthen your frame. You will be like a well-watered garden, like a spring whose waters never fail.
>
> Isa. 58:11

May this indeed be true of your life. May your well-watered garden bear much spiritual fruit for God's glory.

| GEMS |
| --- |
| |

# HELPS FOR LEADERS

## PREPARING TO LEAD

I am delighted that you have chosen this workshop. I remember the growth the women from my home church experienced as we studied God's character through the fruit of the Spirit. I pray that you will richly grow, too.

When we decided to study this material, we divided into groups of five to eight women. We called these G.A.R.D.E.N. groups, which stood for "Give And Receive Discerning Each Need." After all, if you're going to take time from extremely busy schedules to get together, you surely should try to meet needs. Also, we discovered the beauty of receiving—a by-product of our giving to one another. (Therefore, we thought the name both clever and appropriate in light of our growth-oriented study!)

In our GARDEN groups we tried to provide a healthy climate for stimulating growth. Friendliness, openness, faithfulness in attendance, and such a simple thing as creative name tags, enhanced our time together. We always regarded prayer requests with confidentiality. We encouraged all contributions to the discussion, even if they were somewhat off-base; the leader then had the job of tactfully steering the group back on track. We strongly encouraged study preparation. For the leaders it is an absolute must!

Ideally, the GARDEN group leaders contacted the members weekly to keep abreast of any special needs. We set aside time for sharing burdens and prayer requests. We also encouraged keeping prayer notebooks with the date and the request, along with the date and the answer.

Memory work should be emphasized, and rewarded with simple tokens like fruit stickers, garden seeds, herbal teas, bookmarks, potted flowers, or devotional booklets. Develop a fruitful time together; be accountable; make it fun, and keep it simple, yet special.

To enhance the study, you may want to add object lessons from your own life, or your surroundings. Simple suggestions are given in each chapter. Use them to stimulate your own creative thinking.

Before we divided into our specific GARDEN groups, we all met together for a time of praise in song. The leader chose songs which pertained to the quality for that day. (For "love" you could use "Jesus Loves Me" and "Love Him in the Morning"; for "joy" you could sing "I've Got the Joy, Joy, Joy, Joy Down in My Heart" or "Jesus, Others and You," etc.) My sister, Susan Heath, and I, wrote the following song that could be used for your theme song. (As you will note, all nine qualities of the fruit of the Spirit are in this song.)

```
                C           G            C
Chorus: Practice the presence of Jesus,
                F           C            G
        Practice the presence of Christ,
          C     G      C
        Take on God's perspective,
        G                         G⁷
        Let him reign in your life. . . .

                 F
Verse 1: Practice his Goodness,
                 C
         Practice his Love,
           G
         Live in the Joy,
                 C
         That comes from above . . .
                 F
         Practice his Patience,
                 C     Am
         Let his Spirit reign,
             D         G
         Then you will find,
                         F
         That you'll be more Kind,
                 D           G  F  Em  Dm
         Inner Peace you'll attain. . . .

Chorus: Practice the presence of Jesus,
        Practice the presence of Christ,
        Take on God's perspective,
        Let him reign in your life. . . .
```

Verse 2: Practice his Gentleness,
        Be Faithful,
        Obey his Word,
        You'll gain Self-Control,
        Praise his Name,
        Let his Spirit reign,
        Then you will find,
        That you'll have all nine,
        Fruit of the Spirit you'll gain . . .

Chorus: Repeat with variation on second time through.
        *F*                          *C*
        Practice the presence of Jesus,
        *F*                            *G*
        Practice the presence of Christ,
        *C*       *F*
        Take on God's perspective,
        *F*       *C*
        Let him reign in your life.

We emphasized small group study, so we gave the leaders the "Ten Commandments for Leading a Small Group," compiled by Pastor Dave Stout and revised by my husband, Jim Swanson. They are listed below. We will elaborate on one commandment in each chapter of the Helps for Leaders. Hopefully, they will help you, as a leader, to have an enhanced and effective small group study.

### The Ten Commandments for Leading a Small Group

*1.* Know everyone's name; refer to names often.

*2.* Always ask questions that require much thought. Do not ask yes or no questions.

*3.* Always compliment every answer. Do not bluntly reject any answer.

*4.* Moderate the discussion. Do not lecture.

*5.* Develop a "we" mentality. Get the answers from the entire group.

*6.* Know your lesson!

*7.* Do not insist that someone answer a question. Doing so may embarrass the person.

*8.* Side step arguments. Speak to the people later, in private.

*9.* Keep questions simple and clear. No deep theology.

*10.* Do not answer your own questions. Long pauses can be your friends.

Keep this page marked in your book. At home, read it over briefly just before each study. Try one "commandment" at each meeting to improve the way you serve. Do not try every "command" at any one study—it could be overwhelming. You can cover more ground in ten small steps than one large leap!

## 1 / THE FRUIT OF THE SPIRIT

The introductory lesson has a brief overview and outline of the book of Galatians. Here I would like to develop a more in-depth view of the situation in the Galatian church at that time.

The Christians who accepted the Messiah and the new covenant were slipping back into a wrong view of the purpose and nature of the Law. Paul had a high view of the Law, for in Rom. 7:12 he praises Moses' covenant as being "holy, righteous, and good." He also refers to it as a "glorious" thing, though a dim lightbulb compared to the new covenant (2 Cor. 3:1–11).

Though Paul had a high view of the goodness of the Mosaic covenant, he uses every bit of rabbinical wisdom he can muster to show that to go back to it and depend on it for salvation and daily living would be a grave mistake. To go back to the Law would make them airheads (Gal. 3:1). Paul states that to live by this distorted view of the old covenant would be to live by human achievements and therefore nullify the grace of the new covenant. They would be living by the "flesh," and thus subject to God's curse (Gal. 3:10). (Compare Deut. 28–29 for further study.) The law is temporary. Abraham's eternal covenant, arranged beforehand, is lasting (Gal. 3:6–21).

Although the Mosaic covenant was gracious, and not too hard for the Israelites to do (Deut. 31), the Galatians now had the new covenant. Jesus had taken all the curses by hanging on the tree (cross) and left all the blessings for those who came to believe and trust in him (Gal. 3:13–14). Jeremiah predicted this new covenant (Jer. 31:31), that would be internalized in the person who would come to faith. This inward heart-belief is made possible through the outpouring of the Spirit which was given to all Christians at Pentecost.

The indwelling of God through the Holy Spirit gives to Christians the ability to defeat the principle of law that motivates us towards works of human effort, called "fleshly works." Our flesh can cause us to be enslaved and immoral, making our very relationship to God questionable (Gal. 5:16–21). The "fruit" of the Holy Spirit contrasts sharply to this since the Spirit does not enslave us, but frees us to *live*.

Now let's look at the two lists of how a Christian can choose to live. The first list is called "the works of the flesh" or "acts of the sinful nature." This refers to the type of life a person can live when he depends on human achievement to follow the 613 commands that God set up in the Mosaic covenant. Remember, the Law by itself was perfectly right and holy. But when the command is given to obey, the opposite desire surfaces. (See Rom. 7:1–25, especially v. 7.) Provision was made in the old covenant to overcome this opposing desire (Deut. 30:11 ff.).

Then Christ came. God then apparently took away the provision since it was unnecessary once Christ and the new covenant came into effect. Now all that was left from the Law was the desire to do the very opposite of what God wants (Rom. 7:13, 20). This is the "work of the flesh." Fifteen words in Gal. 5:19–21 describe what the practice of the flesh is like. Even this list is not complete, since v. 21 includes the phrase "and the like."

Paul then lists the fruit of the Spirit of God, and in the following weeks we will glean God's truth from each quality. No quality is separate from the others, and the meaning of many of the words overlap (even as they do in other virtue lists in the New Testament). The nine fruit of the Spirit are like a collage of circles overlapping other circles, some within others, some very close, and others barely touching. All are necessary to make the collage complete. As we study how the qualities are unique as well as how they overlap the others, we will discover how to be fruitful women of God.

This lesson reveals why I wrote this workshop: I needed to know God better so that I could face everyday life more victoriously. The main thrust of questions 1–5 is to distinguish between our fallen nature and our new life in Christ.

**1.** and **2.** Works of the flesh (KJV) or acts of the sinful nature (NIV), vs. the fruit of the Spirit

God wanted to show the unity of these benefits flowing from his character. God's Spirit is unified and whenever his Spirit works within a believer's heart many of these qualities will be manifested. In this study you will discover several of these qualities linked together two and three at a time in various passages.

**3.**

| Works of the Flesh | Fruit of the Spirit |
|---|---|
| sexual immorality | love |
| impurity, debauchery | joy |
| idolatry, witchcraft | peace |
| hatred, discord, jealousy | patience |
| fits of rage | kindness |
| selfish ambition | goodness |
| dissensions, factions | faithfulness |
| envy, drunkenness | gentleness |
| orgies and the like | self-control |

**4.** This question is to stimulate creative thinking. Some possible answers are: toil, sweat, self-effort, drudgery, and hardship.

**5.** Possible answers include: conducive climate, plentiful water supply, fertilizer, sunshine, pruning, weeding, proper soil and timing. Don't dwell too long on these answers, as they are just to try to stimulate more discussion in the group.

The importance of questions 6–8 is to help group members recognize that our sinful nature must be crucified, and that it is the Spirit—not our own willpower—that will produce fruit. If we keep feeding on our passions and desires, there will be no room for the Spirit to produce godly qualities. Throughout the study, we will emphasize yielding to God, focusing on God, trusting in God, and knowing his character in order to grow spiritual fruit.

**6.** The sinful nature with its passions and desires

**7.** God's Spirit

**8.** Conceitedness, provoking, and envying one another.

If time permits, read together Ps. 1, John 15, or Matt. 7:16–19.

**9.** Take time to discuss at least one personal goal from each group member.

If time permits, spend time praying for one another's goals. Also, allow time for you to recite together the memory work. As children, we often spend a lot of time in Sunday school rehearsing memory work. As we get older we place less emphasis on such a powerful tool. Therefore, I really want to exhort you to take your memory work seriously! (It's no more than two verses each week.) Try to be accountable to each other, and most of all, to the Lord!

Encourage your group members to write down their own discoveries in the GEMS space. Perhaps they read in their devotional time about one of the qualities of the Spirit found in Gal. 5:22–23. Or maybe they read a passage about bearing fruit, or one that gave them a better handle on what Spirit life is all about. Allow time for them to express what they may be learning independently.

## 2 / LOVE

The First Commandment for Leading a Small Group:

*Know everyone's name; refer to names often.*

Because we each like to be called by our own name, it is crucial for a leader to take special interest in learning her group members' names. We did a very practical thing by making name tags. Some groups wore bright pink heart-shaped tags with calligraphy-lettered names. Others had little stickers on which they penned their names. Some had Bible verses written on theirs. (Because many of the women didn't like having pins poked through their clothes or stickers caught on their sweaters, some of the leaders made tags with long ribbons attached so the women could just slip them over their heads.) These tags were passed out at the beginning of the study and always collected at the end to prevent their being lost.

See to it that new people are introduced before the discussion begins. Contact them during the week after the study and try to get them a name tag by the very next meeting.

As you meet to study love, try to create a spirit of warmth among you. Sometimes soft lighting, soft praise music, and a comfortable chair arrangement can lend a helping hand to group warmth. (Try to have extra chairs available in case additional women arrive. In this way everyone can sit comfortably.) Be sure that in at least your first few weeks you appoint a greeter to give a friendly smile, warm handshake or hug to those coming through the door. A hot mug of herbal tea or hot chocolate can also set a nice tone. (Do be sensitive to dieters and others who may not care for or may be offended by such drinks.)

**1.** Notice how many times these verses talk of God giving or providing of himself. Love is action!

|  | Who | How or Why |
|---|---|---|
| Deut. 7:6–9 | The Israelites | Kept his oath, redeemed them from land of slavery. |
| Neh. 9:16–21 | The Israelites | Forgave them, was gracious, slow to anger, did not abandon them, provided direction and guidance, gave them his good Spirit for instruction, gave manna, sustained them for forty years. |

| | Who | How or Why |
|---|---|---|
| Jer. 31:1–6 | The Israelites | Gave them an everlasting love, will build them up again. |
| Zeph. 3:14–17 | The Israelites | Took away their punishment, turned back their enemies, is with them, quiets them with his love. |
| John 3:16 | The world | Gave his only Son in order to give all believers eternal life. |
| Rom. 5:5–8 | Sinners | Poured out his love into us by the Holy Spirit; Christ died for us. |
| Gal. 2:20 | Paul | Christ loved him and gave himself for Paul. |
| Eph. 2:4–9 | Those dead in transgressions | Made us alive in Christ, gave us his grace. |

**2.** David was a man who truly experienced a deep relationship with his God. He undoubtedly experienced many facets of God's love. Some possible answers are that God is faithful, a constant lover, everlasting, a giver, gracious, unbiased, and sacrificial.

**3.** The personal definitions may include some of the following: God actively and sacrificially bent himself down to each sinner, calling him or her to himself. He graciously forgives in his kind love and provides for his people, remaining constant in his love, regardless of the response.

**4.** They are to love their enemies, pray for them.

**5.** Jesus' followers are to imitate Christ's love. We are to go beyond what the tax collectors do and follow God's example of loving others impartially.

**6.** Love one another as I have loved you.

**7.** We are to model Jesus' love.

**8.** He commanded it so that we would be known as Jesus' followers and disciples.

**9.** He or she will obey Jesus' commands.

**10.** A forever Counselor, the Holy Spirit.

**11.** They will be loved by God; they will see Jesus again.

**12.–14.** If time allows, encourage your group members to share their applications. Often personal sharing is more uncomfortable to do, yet it is that very sharing that creates growth in your group. Set the example by being willing to share your applications.

Practice Ps. 86:15 together, and have GEMS time.

## 3 / MORE LOVE

The Second Commandment for Leading a Small Group:

*Always ask questions that require much thought. Do not ask yes or no questions.*

The questions you ask should indicate adaptability to both the material and the immediate situation. You should always be ready with general questions that will stimulate and guide thinking. Ask questions like: "Do the rest of you agree?" "What do you think this means?" "Can anyone else think of any more ideas along this line?" "What can we learn from this?" "How does this apply to your daily life?" "What is the relationship between these ideas?"

Encourage discussion by asking several people to contribute to a question. "What do the rest of you think?" "Is there anything else to add?" Make a list of such open-ended questions. The list might include: "What do you think this passage means?" "What can we learn from this passage about God, Christ, ourselves, our responsibility, or our relationships to others?'' ''Has this passage ever meant something special to you? If so, why?'' (Be sure the response is correct and in keeping with the passage.) ''What don't you understand about this passage?''

Because we are again focusing on love, perhaps home-made heart-shaped sugar cookies or a heart-shaped cake could whet the group's appetite to learn more about love! (Appoint someone else to provide the goodies. Leaders must not do everything, for then it becomes a one-woman show. Share the work; it will make the group members feel like it is their study too.) Ask your hostess if she has a red tablecloth or a centerpiece with a valentine theme. If you meet at your church, set up a refreshment table or a beverage table with a heart theme. Be creative and fun, and create an atmosphere that will guide the group towards learning.

1. God
2. His only son, Jesus, was the atoning sacrifice.
3. God gave his love through his Spirit.
4. God's love prepares us for the Day of Judgment.
5. Perfect love drives out fear.
6. We must love our brothers; if we hate them, then we don't truly love God.
7. Neither trouble, hardship, persecution, famine, naked-ness, danger, the sword, death, life, angels, demons, present nor future, height nor depth, nor anything else in all creation.
8. It gives us security in God's love.
9. God disciplines and punishes us.
10. Do not make light of it, or lose heart.
11. Personal, varied answers.
12. He laid down his life.
13. Actions and truth are required.
14. I would ask if God's love really was in the church.
15. It pleases the love-giver.
16. God gave the Spirit.

**17.** Love is: patient, kind, not a recorder of wrongs, unfailing, a rejoicer in truth, protecting, trusting, hoping, persevering, the greatest.

Love is not envious, boastful, proud, rude, easily angered, self-seeking, delighting in evil.

**18.** Varied, personal answers.

**19.–22.** Take time to read the love letters to God. Pray about the areas where women have fear or need discipline. Tell how you actively loved someone in need this week. Remember, honest sharing creates close family ties.

Practice 1 John 4:10 together, and have GEMS time.

## 4 / JOY

The Third Commandment for Leading a Small Group:

*Always compliment every answer. Do not bluntly reject any answer.*

Compliment any answer. Respond to even blatantly wrong answers with "I never thought of that" or "That's an interesting response, what do the rest of you think?" A person should not be allowed to feel that she has failed. This is especially true of new members of your study.

Encourage people when they share. Say "Thanks for sharing that with us." This is especially important when someone shares a personal concern or struggle. Show excitement when group members discover something. "That's great," "super insight," and "very good observation" are appropriate comments.

Observe facial expressions. They give away those who disagree with an answer. Ask for their opinion.

Deal with irrelevant issues by suggesting that the purpose

of your study is to discover what is in the lesson. Suggest an informal chat about tangential or controversial issues after the regular study is dismissed.

As this lesson focuses on joy, try to create a "sunny" atmosphere. Yellow paper beverage cups will brighten up the time together. Even though our focus is not outward circumstances, but an inward perspective, a little brightness goes a long way! Spend an extra amount of time in praise songs. Joy is a mindset and as we let praise and worship songs focus our attention on God, our everyday trials may seem less trying.

**1.** There is joy in God's presence. He is our joy and delight!

**2.–4.** God desires to bestow all joy and peace on believers as they trust him through the empowerment of the Holy Spirit.

**5.** and **6.** David was rich in blessings as God made him king; he was glad with the joy of God's presence and victories as he trusted in the Lord.

**7.–9.** After David's adulterous relationship with Bathsheba, he asked God to cleanse, wash, and blot his iniquities from him. We cannot have genuine joy as we wallow in sin. In fact, believers who continually choose to disobey are probably the most frustrated people on earth. After his joy was restored, David desired to teach transgressors God's ways; joy-filled believers are equipped to teach others God's ways not only verbally, but also through their actions—actions that speak loudly and graciously.

**10.** Reasons for the Israelites to have joy:

Deut. 16:13–15: Feast of Tabernacles

1 Kings 8:65–66: Solomon observing the festival, dedication of temple

2 Chron. 30:21–27: Feast of Unleavened Bread

Ezra 6:22: Feast of Unleavened Bread; the Lord filled

them with joy by changing the king of Assyria's attitude.

Neh. 8:10–17: Nehemiah said, "The joy of the Lord is your strength." Nehemiah read the Law before the people on the first day of the seventh month.

**11.** New Testament reasons for joy:

**a.** Jesus is born! Jesus is raised from the dead! Jesus ascends into heaven!

**b.** Jesus is our focus.

**12.–14.** The disciples were instructed to remain in God's love and to obey Jesus' commands. Jesus talked to them, so that his joy could be in them and be completed. Obedience and remaining in Christ's love go hand in hand and result in joy.

**15. and 16.** Paul and Timothy were able to rejoice, even in trials, through the power of God in the Holy Spirit.

**17. and 18.** In order for Paul to have his joy complete, he desired the Philippians to be like-minded, to have the same love, and to be one in Spirit and purpose. A united spirit among your women's Bible study increases joy, and is also a beautiful testimony to newcomers.

**19.–21.** Even though they often do, trials should not affect our joy. The Christian has something, our glorious hope in Christ, which allows us to climb above our seemingly hopeless earthly situations to new levels of joy. Our heavenly perspective does equip us with an inexpressible joy which need not tarnish, even in the worst of trials. Perspective makes all the difference!

**22.** John, the elder, received great joy when he heard of his children walking in the truth.

**23.–27.** Although not often practiced, there can be great healing during confession times. If your group has a particularly close relationship, encourage a time of out-loud confessing. If your group is relatively new to each other, this may be an awkward situation. I would still encourage you to do so, but perhaps do it together silently. Often sin robs us of our joy, so confession is a primary step to a life overflowing with joy. You may want to take some time to discuss what each woman believes is your purpose in meeting together. (You might be surprised to find that some are feeling frustrated because they are not seeing what they feel is important being accomplished.) During the week it is a *must* to write that encouraging note to your spiritual "parent," or to someone who has greatly influenced your Christian walk. Writing that note will not only brighten someone else's day, but I bet it will make you have an extra "Sonny" day, too. Sharing those circumstances that robbed your members of joy, and listening to how they replaced their misdirected feelings with a proper focus may encourage all of you. Try to allow time for this sharing.

Practice Phil. 4:4 together, and have GEMS time.

## 5 / PEACE

The Fourth Commandment for Leading a Small Group:

*Moderate the discussion. Do not lecture.*

Never tell what you can ask! You should personally enter the discussion as little as possible.

The leader must be flexible because the discussion will not go exactly as she has planned. When stuck, you can restate questions in different words. Redirect those questions which are asked you. Say, "That's a good question. What do you think about that, Sherrie?" Remember, a discussion leader is a ping-pong net watching the ball of discussion move between members of the group.

In beginning a discussion, it is best to call upon the more talkative people to keep the discussion moving freely. Once group members are acquainted with one another, this is not necessary. When the talkative ones have talked long enough, bring others into the discussion. Strike a balance between volunteers and shy people.

Since peace is our focus today, take a couple of minutes to do some relaxation exercises, like deep breathing exercises and stretching to the sky exercises. You'd be surprised at how few women take time to relax! (It's good therapy, but be sensitive to those with physical limitations.) Emphasize cool colors by using a soft blue tablecloth or centerpiece for your study area. Emphasize the cross this week as a clear reminder of what a tremendous price was paid to establish our peace.

**1.**

|  | Attribute | Context |
|---|---|---|
| Rom. 15:33 | God of peace | Paul plans to meet Romans; he needs to be rescued from unbelievers in Judea. |
| 1 Cor. 14:33 | God of peace; not of disorder | Confusion about prophecy, tongues, and church orderliness. |
| 2 Cor. 13:11 | God of love and peace | Paul gives final warnings to listen to his counsel and to be of one mind. |
| Phil. 4:9 | God of peace | Put into practice what they have seen in Paul. |
| 1 Thess. 5:23 | God of peace | Final instructions; may God sanctify you. |
| 2 Thess. 3:16 | Lord of peace | Final greetings; may God give you peace at all times and in every way. |

**2. a.** He justified both by faith through the Lord Jesus Christ.

**b.** He made peace through Christ's blood, shed on the cross.

**c.** He is our peace; he has made the two (Jew and Gentile) one. He destroyed the barrier, the dividing wall of hostility, by abolishing the law. He created one new man, reconciling both to God through the cross.

This dividing wall may have been referring to the stone screen in the temple court past which the Gentiles could not go. In fact, if a Gentile did go into the inner courts, he was subject to the death penalty. (See Josephus, Ant. 15, 11, 5; Acts 21:28.)

**3. a.** The Holy Spirit was sent to teach Christ's followers about peace.

**b.** He is still with us today.

**4. a.** Do not let your heart be troubled.

**b.** Do not be afraid.

Trouble and fear can cripple our peace. We need to keep a clear perspective of God's character in full view always!

**5.** God promises perfect peace to the steadfast, trusting mind.

**6.** Consult your dictionaries for definitions. They should include ideas like:

steadfast: firmly fixed in place, immovable, not subject to change.

trusting: depending on; hoping in; relying on; placing your confidence in; to rely on without fear or misgivings.

**7.** The Lord must be our focus, and he is depicted as the Rock eternal.

**8. a.** mind of sinful man

**b.** mind of the Spirit

**9. a.** sinful nature = death; inability to please God

**b.** the Spirit = life and peace

**10.** It is a matter of choice; you cannot always make a

child's choices for him or her, just as God does not enforce right choices on his children. He tells us the best way through his Word, yet he allows us the privilege to decide. As we make right choices to live by the Spirit, peace will reign in our lives.

**11.–13.** Christians must avoid repaying evil for evil. According to the Word, there seems to be *no* situation in which the believer is to retaliate, for it is God who will balance the scale of justice.

**14.–17.** This passage speaks of the cultural situation where eating and drinking food offered to idols was causing fellow Christians to stumble. The three qualities of the kingdom of God are: righteousness, peace, and joy. These are given through the Holy Spirit. As believers, we must aim to do what leads to peace, and what leads to mutual edification.

**18.** Leaders, be especially sensitive to those who may have never experienced inner peace through Christ's work on the cross. What a perfect time to encourage them to seriously consider Christ's claims. Allow time for those who have trusted Christ to publicly praise God for his peace.

**19.** and **21.** Hopefully, these questions have already been dealt with individually during this past week. Perhaps one of the women would like to share a specific area she is dealing with and may need prayer for.

**20.** The ideal answers are

**a.** 5

**b.** 3, 5

**c.** 3

**d.** 1, 4

Practice Phil. 4:6–7 together, and have GEMS time.

## 6 / PATIENCE

The Fifth Commandment for Leading a Small Group:

*Develop a "we" mentality. Get the answers from the entire group.*

Do not personally correct an individual. Let the group come to conclusions and corrections for themselves. By the way, a group can learn a great deal by disagreeing over a passage. Bring group members into the discussion and get their opinions. An individual will take the correction from the group more easily than from the leader. The group should feel the final conclusion is "our" conclusion.

Do not give the impression that you are simply waiting for the group to reach your conclusions, and that once they reach them it is time to move on to the next point. Instead, use brainstorming sessions and buzz groups for variety and stimulation in your discussion group.

When one of your members has reached a faulty conclusion, you may ask her another question, the answer to which will enable her to discover for herself her wrong conclusion. In this way she can discover her mistake, which is better than having you tell her.

As the group focuses on patience this week, it might be insightful for group members to share an event during the past week that was really exasperating. Someone could bring a small saucepan as an object lesson. Each woman could think over the past week's events and could write down on little slips of paper the events which drew on her patience. Those she responded to correctly, she could put inside the pot and those she did not, she could lay outside the pot—as if she had let them boil over.

**1.**

|  | Who | When | How |
|---|---|---|---|
| Exod. 34:4–7 | God said to Moses | After Ten Commandments were given the second time | God maintains his love, forgiving wickedness, rebellion, and sin. |
| Neh. 9:16–18, 29–31 | Nehemiah recalls Israelite history |  | God did not desert them in their sin. |
| Joel 2:12–13 | The Lord through Joel | In prophecy of coming invasions of Judah's enemies | God is slow to anger. |
| Jonah 3:10–4:2 | Jonah states it | After God forgives Ninevah | God did not put an end to them or abandon them. |
| 1 Tim. 1:12–16 | Paul | In letter to Timothy | God showed Paul unlimited patience. |
| 2 Peter 3:9, 15 | Peter | In his warning to believers about false teachers and scoffers | God is patient; waiting for the world to repent. |

**2.**

|  | Patient | Impatient |
|---|---|---|
| Prov. 14:29 | has great understanding | displays folly |
| Prov. 15:18 | calms a quarrel | stirs up dissension |
| Prov. 16:32 | better than a warrior, a taker of a city |  |
| Prov. 19:11 | wisdom gives patience; overlooks an offense |  |
| Prov. 25:15 | can persuade a ruler |  |

**3.–5.** David waited patiently for the Lord. God turned to him, heard his cry, lifted him out of slimy pit—out of mud and mire, sat his feet on a rock, gave him a firm place to stand, and put a new song in his mouth. When God's children wait patiently for him to work in their lives, many will see, and will fear God, and will put their trust in him.

**6.–8.** Abraham responded to God's promises by waiting patiently for him. God in turn did what he promised. This process took at least thirteen years.

**9. a.** In affliction

**b.** As a prisoner for the Lord, Paul admonished readers to be patient in order to live a life worthy of their calling.

**c.** As God's chosen people, we are to be patient in order to bear with each other and forgive.

**d.** With all

**e.** When preaching the Word, when correcting, rebuking, and encouraging

**f.** Until the Lord's coming; stand firm.

**10.** These are conversation questions to stimulate creative thinking. There are no right or wrong answers. Some feel that any kind of anger is wrong. Others feel that it is appropriate for Christians to feel righteous anger, which causes a person to react by taking a positive action to rid one's world of a sinful situation. One thing is certain: angry outbursts of a physical nature are never a characteristic of a patient person. Growing patience is a process; it does take time. It can be a painful process as a person evaluates his or her own shortcomings; however, it should not be purely drudgery. It should be a process in which the person will feel good as he or she trusts in God. It is a process of learning to "Father filter" every situation and quietly rest in it. Growing patience is not just something you grit your teeth and do, but it is a positive choice that results in glorifying your Lord.

**11.–13.** Praise God specifically for the way he has been

patient with you. Share with each other the kinds of circumstances that cause you to falter in this area. Pray specifically for each other about these situations. Perhaps you can spend time in groups of two or three, praying for one another. By mutually sharing and bearing each other's burdens, you will increase your accountability to one another and promote the kind of relationships that please God.

Practice 2 Peter 3:9 together, and have GEMS time.

## 7 / KINDNESS

The Sixth Commandment for Leading a Small Group:
*Know your lesson!*

Be a good scout! Be prepared. Do not give in to the temptation to neglect preparation because the leader is supposed to ask *everyone else* for answers. In fact, your job is greater because you must give direction to the whole of the study. Why are you studying this material? Where is the study going? What is the application? Any guide who does not thoroughly know the woods he or she is hunting in certainly is not worth hiring or following.

Keep your focus. When necessary, tactfully and quickly direct the discussion back to the major issue at hand. Be flexible and skip any questions which do not fit into the discussion as it progresses.

For this lesson, why not surprise your women with a really different centerpiece—a great big Rock. Do you have any clues as to why? In our lesson, David, in 2 Sam., declares God to be the Rock, his Savior, the One who shows unfailing kindness.

**1.** God's kindness:

|  | To Whom | How |
|---|---|---|
| Gen. 32:9–12 | Jacob | He had only a staff—God made him prosper. |
| Gen. 39:20–23 | Joseph | When in prison, God granted him favor with the warden. |
| Ruth 2:19–20 | Ruth | Gave her Boaz |
| 2 Sam. 22:47–51 | David | Avenged him, put nations under him, set him free, exalted him, rescued him, gave him victories. |
| Isa. 63:7–8 | Israel | Became her Savior |

**2.** God's kindness and its effects:

|  | To Whom | Effects |
|---|---|---|
| Luke 6:35 | The ungrateful and wicked |  |
| Rom. 2:3–4 | Man | Leads to repentance |
| Eph. 2:4–7 | Those dead in transgressions | Made us alive |
| Titus 3:3–5 | The foolish, disobedient, deceived, enslaved | Salvation |
| 1 Peter 2:1–3 | Believers (newborn) | Grow up in salvation; develop a craving for the Word. |

**3.–5.** David showed Jonathan's crippled son, Mephibosheth, God's kindness by restoring his family's land to him, and by allowing him to eat at David's table for the remainder of his life.

**6.–10.** A kind word cheers a person. A blessed person

must be kind to the needy for it is a way to please God. To oppress the poor is to show contempt for God. Some practical ways to be kind to the needy are to buy them some groceries, pay their utility bills, pass on some clothes to them, give them gas money to get to a job interview, and give them opportunity to earn some extra money by doing chores for you.

**11.** and **12.** A kind and compassionate person forgives. Christ set this example, and if you are unable to forgive it shows that you have forgotten how great a price God paid in forgiving you.

**13.** and **14.** Bad company corrupts kindness. The saying "garbage in, garbage out" goes along with this idea. If we are influenced only by "bad" input, chances are we will become tainted in our actions. If we ignore God's readily displayed kindness, and never observe other people being kind, we probably will not easily develop this quality in our lives. Think about this in regard to your children. Do you allow them to spend most of their time with kids who are unforgiving, selfish, and sarcastic? Make sure they are being positively influenced with God's character qualities.

**15.–17.** Go around in a circle and share praise to God for his kindness. Spend time praying to God for one another that you all may be truly forgiving in every situation. Take time to share specific areas in which God may have convicted you to change in order to be influenced more by kindness.

**18.** One way to answer the following is:

| Person | What to Give |
| --- | --- |
| a rest home patient | a friendly, drop-in visit |
| a wife-beater | forgiveness |
| a neglected child | a toy or clothes, read a story |
| a family without income | a bag of groceries |
| a person in unbelief | tell them of God's kindness |

a disabled person

a helping hand in doing chores

a depressed person

a cheerful word

Practice Titus 3:4—5 together, and have GEMS time.

## 8 / GOODNESS

The Seventh Commandment for Leading a Small group:

*Do not insist that someone answer a question. Doing so may embarrass the person.*

Don't prod. When a person says that she is not able to answer a question, generally assume this is true.

Ask specific people to answer the study questions. This will keep each woman on her toes. If she stumbles, help her along by clarifying the question. Those who do extra study of the lessons should be able to share their results briefly. Commend them for their efforts.

As we focus on goodness this week, we must remember that God is our standard for goodness. Perhaps a centerpiece with the Word prominently placed in it will be a reminder of 2 Tim. 3:16—17—that through the Word we are equipped for good works. Or, you may want to put together an arrangement of tools to remind your group members that we are God's workmanship created for good works.

**1.** God's goodness:

| | Verses | Actions |
|---|---|---|
| Exod. 33:17–20 | 33:19 | God shows Moses his goodness (mercy, compassion) |
| 1 Chron. 16:1, 7, 23–36 | 16:36 | God brings the Ark of Covenant into David's tent—David speaks of his salvation, marvelous deeds, splendor, holiness |
| 2 Chron. 5:1–3, 11–14 | 5:13 | Solomon dedicates temple; "He is good; his love endures forever." |
| Neh. 9:1–35 | 9:13, 20, 25, 35 | God gave Israelite descendants decrees, commands that are good, good Spirit to instruct, they ate to the full, were well-nourished. They revelled in God's goodness; great goodness in the spacious fertile land. |
| Ps. 118:1, 29 | 118:1, 29 | He is good. His love endures forever |

**2.** and **3.** God has a good, pleasing, and perfect will. As we renew our minds through the Word, our transformed thinking will be sensitized to his will for us.

**4.–6.** They prayed that God would count the Thessalonians worthy of his calling and that they, by his power, would fulfill every good purpose and act. By doing so, they would glorify the Lord Jesus Christ.

**7.** By allowing God's Word to teach, rebuke, correct, and train us in righteousness, we will be equipped for every good work.

**8.–10.** The older women should teach the younger women what is good: to love their husbands and children, to be self-controlled and pure, busy at home, to be kind, and to be subject to their husbands, so that no one will malign the Word of God.

**11.–13.** By faith we have been saved. We are now God's workmanship created to do good works in Christ Jesus.

**14.** and **15.** The Lord Jesus Christ and God our Father will encourage and strengthen us in our good words and deeds, and it is to them we must look for eternal encouragement and good hope.

**16.–18.** We are to spur one another on to love and good deeds in God. When we maintain a clean conscience and clear perspective of the hope that is in us, we have a greater ability to do so.

**19.** and **20.** Through Jesus we can offer our God a sacrifice of praise. When our perspective is godly, and when we follow the Word to share with others, goodness will flow.

**21.** and **22.** We must abstain from sinful desires in order to live good lives; as a result of a good life, God will be glorified.

**23.–26.** God called us out of his glory and goodness, equipping us with his divine power so that we have everything we need for life and godliness. To our faith we must add goodness, then knowledge, self-control, perseverance, godliness, brotherly kindness, and love. If we have these qualities developing in us, we will be effective and productive in our knowledge of him. If we do not have these qualities, however, we have forgotten that we have been cleansed from our past sins.

**27.–31.** Share specific instances of God's goodness to you. What has he given you that you are especially thankful for? How did you do on rating your time in the Word? Pray for one another that you will make Scripture reading a priority in your lives. Spur one another on to good works by having each woman relate how her or someone else's good works have affected her life. Was anyone won to Christ by a fellow Christian's good works? How have you effectively used good works to bring someone to Christ? Sharing specifics will help bond your relationships with one another. Try to leave enough time for each woman to share one principle on "To teach what is good."

Practice Ps. 118:1 together, and have GEMS time.

## 9 / FAITHFULNESS

The Eighth Commandment for Leading a Small Group:

*Side step arguments. Speak to the people later, in private.*

Keep the discussion non-argumentative by directing questions to the rest of the group. Don't let people who probe become a threat. Learn to say, "I never thought of that . . . " And be sure to utilize your sense of humor in an appropriate manner.

When people or points of view are at obvious loggerheads, run "interference" by saying, "Well, there is obviously more than one thought on this subject. Let's put this on hold for now and move on to the next point." This may be one time the leader must definitely grab the reins of the discussion. Remember, if you don't run "interference," probably no one else will. Experience has shown that to do so before an argument gets out of hand will save time and make the study more profitable.

Disagree agreeably. A saying goes like this: "Those who give harsh words write them in sand. Those who receive harsh words cast them in bronze." Therefore, do not allow your discussions to become argumentative.

As we focus on faithfulness this week, I am reminded that God is faithful and just to forgive us and to cleanse us from all unrighteousness. Perhaps a tablecloth of pure white with a centerpiece of bars of soap and washcloths will remind your group members of this aspect of God's faithfulness.

**1.** God's faithfulness:

| | To Whom | How |
|---|---|---|
| Gen. 32:9–12 | Jacob | Made Jacob prosper |
| Exod. 34:4–8 | Moses | Was faithful to his people. Maintains his love and forgives |
| Deut. 31:30–32:4 | Moses | By being a faithful God who does no wrong |
| Neh. 9:1, 32–35 | The Israelites | While they did wrong, God was faithful and gave them a spacious and fertile land. |
| Ps. 33:4 | Psalmist | By being faithful in all he does |
| Ps. 57:1–3 | David | Gave David refuge, fulfilled his purpose in David; saved him and sent his love. |
| Isa. 25:1 | Isaiah | God has done marvelous things. |
| Isa. 61:8–9 | God's people | He rewards and makes an everlasting covenant; their descendants will be known among the nations. |
| Lam. 3:19–24 | Jeremiah | His compassions never fail; he did not consume his people. |

**2. a.** God has enriched Christians in every way and given them spiritual gifts. He will keep them strong and blameless.

**b.** Provides a way for the tempted believer to stand up under temptation.

**c.** He will keep believers sanctified and blameless.

**d.** He strengthens and protects believers from the evil one.

**e.** God promised us hope and he is faithful.

**f.** He is the faithful Creator.

**g.** He is faithful and just to forgive sins and to purify us from all unrighteousness.

**h.** Jesus is the faithful witness.

**3.** Verses 1, 2, 5, 8, 14, 24, 33, and 49.

**4.** and **5.** Joshua told the Israelites to throw away the gods of the other nations in order to show faithfulness to God.

**6.** and **7.** God's followers must be faithful with material things. Trustworthiness is characteristic of a faithful person and vice versa.

**8.** and **9.** Those teaching about God must be faithful. They must be faithful in their motives for teaching.

**10.–12.** Deacon's wives must be faithful, worthy of respect, not malicious talkers, but temperate and trustworthy. A faithful woman will not talk maliciously, and temperance will frame her life-style. She will be well respected.

**13.** and **14.** We must be faithful in serving the body of Christ by using our spiritual gifts for God's honor.

**15.** Publicly praise God for his faithfulness in your life. What aspect of his faithfulness encourages you most?

**16. a.** As mothers, we must be faithful to what we tell our children. They will misunderstand their significance to us if we are overburdened with ministries. As a result, they end up with a bitter picture of God. Once Carol finds her son, she could sit down with him and confess to him that she is sorry for not keeping her word.

**b.** Try to be faithful to your word. If you cannot make it to an event once you have committed yourself to it, be sure to let the person know. Even if you honestly forget some commitment, be sure to send your apologies so that you set the record straight.

**c.** The old line about "Would you pray about my friend's problems?" is an age-old cover-up for sin—gossiping. We must be women faithful to our friend's honesty and not divulge private matters.

**d.** Being faithful in our thought lives is very important to God. Perhaps you should replace romance novels with other worthwhile reading material.

**e.** Faithful stewardship is essential in our materialistic society. Don't settle for second best. Honor God with your first fruits. That is easier if you do not overextend yourself financially—no matter what your good intentions are. Don't get sucked into the world's mold of owning material goods at the expense of excluding God from your giving. It is too high a price to pay.

**f.** God gave his children spiritual gifts so that they would be equipped to serve. Use them for God's intended use. When you are not faithful in this area, your spiritual life just sits and sours.

**17.** You may want to take time to specifically pray for one another's area of need.

Practice Deut. 32:4 together, and have GEMS time.

## 10 / GENTLENESS

The Ninth Commandment for Leading a Small Group:

*Keep questions simple and clear. No deep theology.*

The group should be able to grasp quickly the meaning of your questions. Questions should always be asked in a way that indicates that they can be answered by anyone. Use another version when a verse is not clear. The discussion leader's lack of clarity—"a spiritual mist"—can create a "fog" for the group.

As we focus on gentleness this week, I am reminded of the

saying, "as gentle as a lamb." Perhaps lamb-shaped sugar cookies or a centerpiece of little sheep might serve as a helpful object lesson. Another idea is to focus on the inner beauty of a gentle and quiet spirit. You may want to put a mirror with a Bible open to 1 Peter 3:3−4 on the middle of your study table.

**1.−3.** In all three passages, Christ is characterized by gentleness. Gentleness definitely does not equal pansiness!

**4.** Moses confronted Pharaoh, led the Israelites out of Egypt, stood before God as intermediary between God and his people, and did other "unwimpy" acts.

**5.** Gentleness exhortations:

| | Who | When | What or How |
|---|---|---|---|
| Gal. 6:1 | The spiritual person | Someone is caught in a sin | Restore him gently. |
| Eph. 4:1−3 | The Ephesians | All the time | Be completely humble, gentle, and patient; bear with one another. |
| Phil. 4:4−5 | The Philippians | Always | Rejoice; let your gentleness be evident to all. |
| 1 Thess. 2:7−9 | Paul, Silas, Timothy | When they were with the Thessalonians | They were gentle like a nursing mom; they loved them and shared their lives with them. |
| 1 Tim. 6:11−12 | Timothy | | Pursue righteousness, godliness, faith, love, endurance, and gentleness; fight the good fight of faith. |
| 2 Tim. 2:22−26 | Timothy | When opposed | Gently instruct; hope for their repentance. |

| | Who | When | What or How |
|---|---|---|---|
| Titus 3:1–2 | People of Crete | | Be obedient, ready to do whatever is good; slander no one, be peaceable, considerate and show true humility. |
| James 1:19–21 | Dear brothers | | Humbly accept the Word planted in you. |
| James 3:13 | The wise and under-standing | | Live a good life; do deeds in the humility that comes from wis-dom. |
| 1 Peter 3:15–16 | | Always be prepared to witness | With gentleness and respect, keeping a clear conscience |

**6.** 1 Peter 3:15–16

**7.** Gal. 6:1

**8.** James 1:19–21

**9.** and **10.** God considers a gentle and quiet spirit to be a beauty that does not fade. As we seek purity, and revere and submit to our husbands, we can develop this unfading beauty.

**11.** Take time to publicly praise God for his example of gentleness.

**12.** Go around in a circle and share a specific situation in which you each displayed gentleness. Use the mentioned situations to stimulate your thinking.

**13. a.** and **b.** There are no right or wrong answers for these creative thinking questions. A gentle person may or may not speak out of turn, but in either case, her manner would include the gentleness of a nursing mom. She would not respond in a prideful or boastful manner, but with humility laced with respect and consideration. To answer question

13b, consider this: would Moses have made a good military sergeant? Yes, I believe so.

We must remove the pansiness out of our English definition for gentleness. Yes, indeed, a gentle person can lead people, and he or she can do it with great care, with strength that pursues patience, with endurance and peaceful harmony.

**14.** Spend time praying with one another about your commitment to the Word. You must catch the vision that your whole spirituality hinges on your knowledge of the Holy One and his Word. You must feast on his Word to keep an eternal perspective of the hope that is in you, and to know how to live in obedience to him.

Spend time practicing Matt. 11:28–29 together, and have GEMS time.

## 11 / SELF-CONTROL

The Tenth Commandment for Leading a Small Group:

*Do not answer your own questions. Long pauses can be your friends.*

Your group members will need time to think about your questions. So allow a person sufficient time to answer and do not be impatient. Asking questions at a rapid pace, leaving insufficient time for answers will distract your group members rather than help them develop their thinking skills. Waiting for answers shows interest and concern for the person asked.

If you get no response at all after a significant period of time, then rephrase the question and try again. Do not be too quick to disregard a question only because there is no immediate response.

In the lesson on self-control we are taught about the importance of being alert and of belonging to the day (rather than the night). How about a centerpiece of an alarm clock with a bright yellow sun under it to try to get this point across? Also, one of the group members could make a bright, round, yellow, or lemon cake to represent the daytime sun. (Unless, of course, your women struggle in the area of overeating! Then why not a plate of nice round yellow pineapple slices?)

**1. a.** Joseph controlled his joy and excitement in seeing his brothers.

**b.** Haman, although filled with rage that Mordecai did not show respect for him, restrained himself.

**2.–5.** Jesus has the power to bring everything under his control. As we remember that our true citizenship is in heaven, it will motivate us to make correct, godly choices. Jesus himself, who has the power to bring everything under his control, will transform our lowly bodies.

**6. a.** reckless words pierce

**b.** without it, you become poor

**c.** eat more than the right amount and you will vomit

**d.** without it, you are like a city with broken down walls

**e.** the foolish man gives full vent to his anger; the wise man keeps control

**7.–9.** The mind of the sinful man battles against the mind controlled by the Spirit. The sinful mind is death; the Spirit-controlled mind is life and peace. The Holy Spirit equips each Christian with the ability to live a Spirit-controlled life. Submission to God and his Spirit enhances our self-control by helping us to make right choices towards holiness.

**10.** and **11.** Those who are unmarried and widows are instructed to marry if they burn with passion.

**12.–14.** God calls us to be holy, thus we must avoid sexual immorality. As we have a mindset toward holiness, a separateness from the world, we can develop self-control and gain control over our desires.

**15.** During persecution, Paul admonishes the Thessalonians to be alert to temptation and to be self-controlled.

**16.** Day is characterized by light, alertness, and self-control. Night is characterized by darkness, sleeping, and drunkenness.

**17.** As Christians, put on the breastplate of faith and love and the helmet of the hope of salvation to win the battle for self-control. As we focus on our faith, the love God gives us, and the hope we have in Christ, our worldly, self-centered desires will have less appeal. Our perspective determines what will have its grip on us.

**18.–20.** The older women are to teach the younger women what is good. They are to love their husbands and children and are to be self-controlled, pure, busy at home, kind, and subject to their husbands. God's gracious salvation teaches us to say no! to ungodliness and worldly passions and to live self-controlled, upright, godly lives. If we are not living a life of self-control perhaps we have forgotten that we have a blessed hope and are Jesus' redeemed people.

**21. and 22.** In order to be self-controlled we must prepare our minds for action; we must focus our hope on grace. We must keep foremost in our thoughts our hope of some day seeing Christ revealed. We are to conform our lives to the holiness of Christ, and to stay away from the evil desires that we once had in our ignorance.

**23. and 24.** We can enhance our prayer lives by being clear minded, self-controlled, and alert. When we are alert, we are more capable of being self-controlled. When we let our defenses down, it's more likely we may let temptations overcome us.

**25.** and **26.** Take a moment to focus together on God's holiness. Praise God for the Spirit he has given to each of us so that we can make right choices. Ask God to help you to submit your will over to him—daily—this week. Discuss which areas of self-control snag you the most. Spend time praying specifically for each woman's particular area of need concerning self-control. Take home with you the name of one group member and her specific area of need so that you may better pray for her this week. Be accountable to the woman who is praying for you, too.

**27.** Depending upon the dynamics of your group, you may want to let the women work on this question silently, without group discussion.

Practice 1 Peter 1:13 together, and have GEMS time.

## 12 / A WELL-WATERED GARDEN

Well, it's your last lesson. What ideas do you have for making it special? You could have a basket full of luscious fruit for a centerpiece. Give flower seedlings to each group member, or packets of seeds, or a colorful plate of sliced fruit—let your own creative juices flow! Perhaps you could take this meeting time to publicly recognize those group members who have faithfully attended, or faithfully prepared, or faithfully memorized Scripture. (It has often been my experience that the studies start out with a lot of enthusiasm and then start to dwindle; that's why it's important to recognize those who have held strong to their commitment.)

**1.** Love, joy, peace, patience, kindness, goodness, faithfulness, gentleness, self-control

**2.** Memory work

**3. a.** Patience
**b.** Faithfulness
**c.** Kindness
**d.** Self-control
**e.** Joy
**f.** Gentleness
**g.** Goodness
**h.** Love
**i.** Peace
**4. a.** Gentleness
**b.** Love
**c.** Faithfulness
**d.** Goodness
**e.** Peace
**f.** Joy
**g.** Faithfulness
**h.** Kindness, Patience
**i.** Goodness
**j.** Patience
**k.** Self-control
**l.** Love
**m.** Kindness
**n.** Peace
**o.** Patience
**p.** Gentleness
**q.** Self-control
**r.** Joy

Practice Isa. 58:11 together, and have GEMS time.